Learn JavaScript Quickly

A Complete Beginner's Guide to Learning JavaScript, Even If You're New to Programming

{CodeQuickly}

CodeQuickly.org

Table of Contents

This page intentionally left blank.

Chapter 1: What is Programming?

Introduction

Have you ever written a program for your computer? If you have, you are off to a good start. You may want to skim this chapter, but you can probably skip to the next one if you would like.

To put it simply, a program is a set of instructions that tells your computer what to do. This sounds simple enough, right? You'd like the computer to send an email, draw a circle, or turn on the oven. Sadly, a computer, even that super powerful chip in your cell phone, does not understand instructions like these. You have to break it down into very simple steps.

Algorithms

The steps that a computer needs to take are expressed in the form of an **algorithm**. This is just a fancy word for a detailed description of steps. Let's consider an algorithm for a simple everyday non-computer task.

Suppose you want to write an algorithm for making a cup of coffee. This might seem silly because it is so simple. All you have to do is:

1. *Make coffee*
2. *Pour into cup*

But we're missing some steps. To make coffee (with a common household coffeemaker), we actually may have to:

1. *Get out the coffee*
2. *Open the can*
3. *Put water in the coffeemaker*
4. *Add coffee to the coffeemaker*
5. *Turn the coffeemaker on*
6. *Wait until done*
7. *Get a cup*
8. *Pour coffee into the cup*

9. Add cream and sugar, if wanted

This is getting complicated! And we haven't considered everything. How much water do we add? How much coffee? In fact, what if we are *out* of coffee?

At its lowest level, for a program to be understandable, the computer needs all of these details and more. The most basic steps in a computer program might look like some of the following examples:

1. *Load 72 into register 1*
2. *Copy memory location 49385 into register 2*
3. *Subtract register 2 from register 1*
4. *If the result is less than zero, go to instruction 42*

Each of these steps may be represented by a single **machine instruction**. When stored in the computer memory, these instructions are expressed in a primitive language to allow the computer to understand them. A typical machine instruction might look like this:

0110 1100 0011 1110 0101 1001 1100 0100

What in the world does this even mean? Fortunately, unless you are a computer architect or a systems programmer, you don't really need to know. Instead, you can instruct the computer using a much more user-friendly **programming language**.

Programming Languages

Early programmers indeed had to write programs using tedious instructions like those listed above. As programs became larger and more complex, it became almost impossible to write them in this way. New languages that would be easier for programmers to understand and write programs in were necessary. The first of such languages that appeared were called **assembly languages**. These provided compact notations for each machine instruction, such as:

LDI R1, 72

```
        LD R2, 49385
        SUB R2, R1
        BLZ, 42
```

This was better than writing 1's and 0's, but not by much. Assembly languages were very hard to learn and understand. The assembly language for Computer X was totally different than the assembly language for Computer Y. There was still a need for more powerful languages that could express complex algorithms in a form that both the computer and the human programmer could understand. The result was the birth of "high-level" programming languages.

The first programming language to achieve widespread use was called FORTRAN, which stands for FORmula TRANslation. This language was developed by IBM to write programs that performed complex numerical calculations. Here is a brief FORTRAN program to test whether a number is even or odd:

```
        INTEGER INUM, IREM
        READ (5,50) INUM
50      FORMAT (I5)
        IREM = INUM - (INUM/2)*2
        IF (IREM.EQ.0) GO TO 200
100     WRITE (6,101) INUM
101     FORMAT(I5,7H IS ODD)
        GO TO 300
200     WRITE (6,201) INUM
201     FORMAT(I5,8H IS EVEN)
300     STOP
```

If you think this looks complex and hard to understand, you are correct. But it is far better than writing individual machine instructions directly. More so, programs written in FORTRAN could run on many different types of computers. We will soon see how.

Early programming languages tried to express algorithms in a format which could be easily understood by both the programmer and the computer. However, programmers still had a lot to learn to be able to understand and write programs like this.

Many other languages were developed after FORTRAN. Some of the most notable ones included COBOL, Pascal, and C. The C language turned out to be especially important, as it was designed to work with the Unix operating system (and later Linux). It also became the inspiration for important present-day languages including C++, Java, and JavaScript.

Here is a program written in C that does the same thing as the FORTRAN program above. This still may look peculiar, but it is a lot easier to understand than the FORTRAN program:

```c
#include <stdio.h>
int main()
{
    int value;
    printf("Enter a value: ");
    scanf("%d", &value);
    if (value % 2 == 0){
        printf("%d is even\n", value);
    } else {
        printf("%d is odd\n", value);
    }
}
```

Well over a thousand programming languages have been developed, and dozens are currently in widespread use. Why not just use a natural language, such as English? It would be nice to write something like:

1. Ask for a number
2. Read the number
3. Divide the number by 2
4. If there is a remainder, print "number is odd"
5. Otherwise, print "number is even"

Unfortunately, this is already too complex for a computer to understand. Moreover, statements in a natural language like this can be ambiguous. Consider the simple sentence:

The man saw the boy with the telescope.

This seems to have clear meaning, until you think a little harder. Who had the telescope, the man or the boy? Perhaps the man was looking through the telescope, or perhaps the boy was carrying it. The sentence doesn't make this clear. Humans will automatically consider the context of the sentence: what do other nearby sentences say? But it is not easy for computers to do this. Programming languages are designed to avoid (or minimize) such problems.

Language Translation

A program written in a programming language cannot be understood by computers directly. Instead, we need to provide a **translator program** to read the original program and produce a version that the computer can understand. Since we are adding a translation step, it is possible to translate the same program to run on different computers, with little or no change to the program itself.

The traditional translator program for programming languages is called a **compiler**. In its simplest form, a compiler reads a program written in a programming language (usually from a file), then outputs the program in a form that the computer understands. The original program is called the **source program**, and the compiler output is called the **executable program**. The executable program is stored in a file until needed. It can then be loaded into the memory and ran or executed.

In practice, a compiler usually translates the source program into an intermediate form, sometimes called the **object program**, which is later processed by a different translator to produce the executable. This provides several benefits, including the ability to combine your program with other programs and libraries that may be provided by the operating system.

In practice, programmers often develop programs using an **Integrated Development Environment**, or **IDE**. An IDE takes care of many of the translation steps automatically, so you may not even be aware of what is happening. You will learn about IDEs for JavaScript in the next chapter.

Most languages developed over the years are designed to be compiled. This includes FORTRAN, Pascal, C, C++, Java, and hundreds of others.

A different translation process has become popular for some recent languages. This process uses an **interpreter** instead of a compiler. The interpreter reads a source program a little at a time and immediately executes that portion. There is no separate intermediate or executable program. The language must be designed so that each small portion can be executed immediately, without waiting to see what the whole program contains. A language like this is sometimes called a **scripting language**.

One scripting language that has become popular in recent times is Python. Another example is JavaScript, the language we focus on in this book.

What would a JavaScript program look like to test whether a number is even or odd? Here is one possibility:

```javascript
var value = prompt("Enter a value: ");
if (value % 2 == 0) {
    document.write(value + " is even\n");
} else {
    document.write(value + " is odd\n");
}
```

As you see, this is very similar to the C program, but there are actually some very important differences. Now that you have an idea what programming is all about, let's plunge into to the next chapter and meet JavaScript itself.

Chapter 2: What is JavaScript?

At this point, you have an idea of what programming is and you may have even written programs in another programming language. Computer programs have been written in hundreds of different languages. Most of these languages are designed to write programs that run directly on your computer (or mobile device) to perform tasks such as writing letters, producing video, compute your taxes, or control your thermostat.

JavaScript arose from a different need and has some important differences from most other programming languages. Let's see what JavaScript is all about.

Background

In the 1990s, the Internet appeared, and the World Wide Web was born. Early web pages were beautiful (sometimes), but static. They could display pictures, text, and sometimes even multimedia, but they could not respond to user actions like typing text or pressing buttons. A popular early web page is shown below.

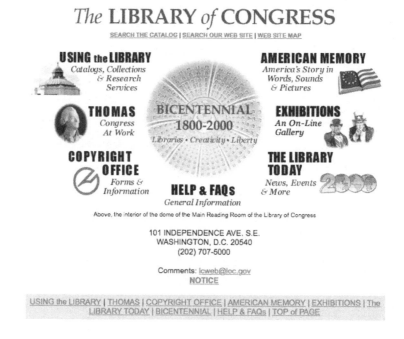

Figure 2-1: An early web page

Web pages are sent to a client computer (e.g., your laptop) over the internet from a remote server. These pages contain data expressed in the **HyperText Markup Language (HTML)**. You may know a lot about HTML already. Don't worry if you are not familiar with it.

HTML is read and interpreted by a program on the client computer called a browser. You are probably familiar with browsers such as Firefox, Chrome, Safari, or Internet Explorer. Each of these use HTML instructions to properly display the text and images from the page on your particular computer display.

Interacting with web pages

In the early days of the Internet, web pages often contained hyperlinks that, when clicked, sent requests for other web pages to the appropriate server. This was the only type of interaction that web pages offered at the time. This was very useful, but what if it was possible to interact with web pages in the same way we interact with local programs using a graphic user interface? A web page could then be viewed as a remotely hosted program, which could be controlled by typing or pressing buttons, just as we would do with local programs in a similar window.

The browser is a local program so this could be done in several ways. One solution would be for the browser to respond to clicks or data input by sending a request to the server, causing a new version of the web page to be sent back to the client. This could work, but would be extremely inefficient, especially on a slow network.

If the browser could request updates for just a portion of the page, leaving the rest as is, performance would improve. For example, if the web page displays a table, individual elements in the table could be updated by the server. This is sometimes a good solution, but other times it is still too cumbersome. What if the desired interaction doesn't require any information from the server? Perhaps it is a simple calculation or a graphic animation.

In this case we would like to be able to run a program on the client computer that does everything we need when that button is clicked. But where does that program come from? It must be supplied by the server, along with the web page.

These ideas were first explored by Netscape Communications, developers of the first commercial web browser, Netscape Navigator. Netscape worked with Sun Microsystems, developers of the Java programming language, to create a method for packaging small Java programs, termed **applets.** These mini programs were delivered from a web server to a client along with a web page. Java was designed to be highly portable, so the same Java program could run on most computer types. An applet could provide things such as a small animation or an interactive calculator. This was done by simply running the applet on the client's machine.

Although useful, Java applets led to several problems, especially the problem of security risks. Once loaded on a client's computer, applets were run by an independent Java interpreter separate from the web browser. An applet could theoretically access data, files and other resources that it was not authorized to use. It was difficult to secure these applets to ensure that they could do only what was intended.

To help resolve this problem, and perhaps improve performance, Netscape began work on a purely interpreted or *scripting* language designed specifically to bring interaction to web pages. Because many web programmers were already familiar with Java, the new language was given a similar name – JavaScript – and a similar syntax. But in other ways, JavaScript would become something very different.

A First Example

We have seen where JavaScript comes from and what it is often used for. But what does a JavaScript program look like? To answer this, let's write a simple program and run it.

Here is a very basic JavaScript program, consisting of one line that displays a welcome message:

```
document.write('Welcome to JavaScript!');
```

Most languages would require at least a couple of extra lines to make a complete program. JavaScript does not. However, we want to use a browser to interpret this program, and to do that we need to make it part of a web page. A complete HTML web page, which does nothing but run our JavaScript program, looks like this:

```
<html>
 <body>
  <script>
   document.write('Welcome to JavaScript!');
  </script>
 </body>
</html>
```

The codes enclosed by <> are HTML tags. In HTML, each element begins with a tag such as <xxx>, and most end with a matching closing tag such as </xxx>. Tags may be nested. Finally, the special tags <script> ... </script> are used to enclose JavaScript programs. For now, this is all we need to know about HTML.

This script is written between the tags `<body>` and `</body>`. This means it will run automatically as soon as the page is loaded. Later we will see how to write scripts to run only when the user takes some action on the page.

Type this program into a text editor such as Notepad or TextPad and save it in a file called `welcome.html`. If you have a HTML editor or a web development environment, by all means use it. But don't use a word processor, which adds lots of hidden things that your browser doesn't like!

Other languages need a compiler to translate programs to native code, or a run-time interpreter to read the program and make it work. JavaScript requires only an interpreter, which is built into your browser.

Run your browser and open the file you just created by selecting **File/Open** or by dragging the file onto the browser. You should see the following output:

```
Welcome to JavaScript!
```

You've created and run your first JavaScript program!

What if you see nothing? In this case, your browser might have JavaScript disabled. This is sometimes done for security reasons. It is rarely necessary today, but it still can be done. If your JavaScript is disabled, you will need to enable it before going further with these examples. The way to do this depends on your specific configuration. You may need to consult the administrator for your computing system.

If this doesn't solve the problem, check for typos in the file. Punctuation is very important, and a missing or incorrect character could cause an error.

Although JavaScript programs can be embedded in HTML code, it is good practice to place them in separate files. These files can then be referred to by the HTML program. The usual file extension used for JavaScript code is `.js`.

To make this change, we can take just the JavaScript line from the above program and place it in a new file called `welcome.js`:

```
document.write('Welcome to JavaScript!');
```

Now we need a new test file to run this example. We can call it `jstest.html`:

```
<html>
 <body>
  <script src=welcome.js></script>
 </body>
</html>
```

Place the HTML file and the JavaScript file in the same directory, then run the HTML file. You should get the same result as before. We will organize most of our JavaScript examples like this from now on.

Editors and IDEs

As noted above, JavaScript programs, along with HTML content, can be written and edited using simple text editors, as long as the editors can output programs as a simple sequence of characters with no extraneous information. Enhanced text editors such as Notepad++ or BBEdit are good choices since they can help check the syntax of JavaScript programs along with many other types of files. Word processors cannot usually be used because they add extra formatting information to the file.

Many programs in other languages are primarily developed using Integrated Development Environments (IDEs) such as Visual Studio or Eclipse. These environments combine editing with compiling or interpreting, testing and debugging, as well as various analysis tools. It is possible to use some of these environments for JavaScript but remember that JavaScript development is a part of web development.

You will need an environment that is designed for development of HTML and CSS along with JavaScript. Popular examples include AWS Cloud9 and Adobe Dreamweaver. Another good option for writing and testing JavaScript is Brackets. Brackets is a source code editor with an emphasis on web development. It is a free software for download developed by Adobe that has live editing features for HTML, CSS and JavaScript.

Remember, if you use a simple text editor, you can run and test your web client-based JavaScript code in almost any browser. The browser provides the JavaScript interpreter and runtime system. Additionally, if your program misbehaves, most browsers are equipped with tools that can be used for web page analysis.

JavaScript Versions

JavaScript has evolved through several versions since the first was incorporated into Netscape Navigator in 1993. A few years later JavaScript was submitted to the European Computer Manufacturers Association (ECMA) for consideration as a standard. This effort led to the publication of the standard ECMA-262, known as ECMAScript, in 1997.

Since then, JavaScript has been viewed as an implementation of ECMAScript. The standard has evolved through several versions, notably the definition of ECMAScript 5, or ES5 in 2009. ES5 was also approved as a standard by the International Organization for Standardization (ISO). More recently, the standard has begun to have annual revisions producing versions such as ES-2015, ES-2016, and ES-2017.

Each new version of ECMAScript/JavaScript has introduced a few new features that were not supported by all browsers, at least for a while. Since 2016, almost all browsers implement ES6, also known as ES-2015. This is the version we will use for all discussions and examples, until stated otherwise in a later chapter of this book.

Using the Language

The original purpose for JavaScript was to write programs that could be sent from a web server to a client computer, along with web pages to be run on the client's browser. This is called **client-side programming**. This is still by far the most common usage.

Client-side JavaScript programs interact with HTML elements on a web page such as text, images, and buttons. JavaScript can locate, examine, and change HTML elements using the HTML **Document Object Model**, or the DOM. You will learn more about this model in a future chapter.

More recently, the potential of JavaScript for other programming applications has been recognized. One important new use is for **server-side programming**. In this case, JavaScript programs that remain on the web server can perform complex functions on behalf of clients, even those that disable JavaScript for security reasons. This is enabled primarily by a package named Node.js, which creates its own virtual server inside the actual web server.

Finally, JavaScript is starting to be used in some applications that are completely separated from web programming. The language is beginning to be recognized as a full general-purpose programming language.

Chapter 3: Rules of the Road

Now we know where JavaScript comes from and have some ideas of what a JavaScript program looks like. It is time to look more closely at some of the details of the language.

A New Example

Here is a slightly more extended example of a JavaScript program. This program displays a textbox that allows the user to enter a number, then prints the square of that number. The number must be between 1 and 10. Type this program into a file called `square.js` and set the file as the target of your `jstest.html` file using the script tag like we did with `welcome.js` in Chapter 2. When you are finished, open `jstest.html` with your browser, and try it out:

```javascript
// Get an input number
var inputNum = prompt("Type a number between 1 and 10");

// If valid, display its square
if (inputNum >= 1 && inputNum <= 10) {
 document.write("The square of " + inputNum + " is " +
      inputNum*inputNum);
} else {
 document.write("Invalid number!");
}
```

When the page opens in a browser, a pop-up window will appear requesting a number between 1 and 10. If you enter 5, for example, the pop-up window should close, and the browser will display the following message:

```
The square of 5 is 25
```

Notice that the message appears on a new page. Now, restart the program and try some other inputs such as 12, 5.2, abc, or nothing at all. What happens in each of these cases?

This is a small program, but we can learn a lot about JavaScript syntax from it. Some things you may find very similar to other languages, and some may be different.

Statements

First, a program is composed of **statements**. Here are two statements from the program above:

```
1. var inputNum = prompt("type a number between 1 and 10");

2. document.write("The square of " + inputNum + " is " +
        inputNum*inputNum);
```

Statements direct the computer to do something. The first statement is an assignment statement, which you will meet later. The second is an output statement, which you have already seen.

In many programming languages, each statement must end with a semicolon. JavaScript does not specifically require a semicolon at the end of each statement. If the semicolon is omitted, the end of the line will signal the end of the statement in most cases. However, using semicolons is good practice and most languages require it. Semicolons make your code more readable and we will continue to use them throughout the remainder of this book.

Long statements in JavaScript can be split between lines (at suitable places). Short statements can be grouped on the same line, as long as they are separated by semicolons:

```
var quantity = 10; var price = 3.50;
```

Spaces between elements in a statement are ignored. The following lines are the same:

```
price=3.50;
price=3.50      ;
```

Of course, we cannot write:

```
price=3. 50;
```

Because spaces *within* elements would confuse the interpreter.

This is also a statement:

```
if (inputNum >= 1 && inputNum <= 10) {
  document.write("The square of " + inputNum + " is " +
```

```
        inputNum*inputNum);
} else {
  document.write("Invalid number!");
}
```

The **if-else** statement takes certain actions depending on a condition. We will learn more about this soon. The important thing to see right now is that some statements can contain other statements in the form of **statement blocks** such as:

```
{

    document.write("Invalid number!");

}
```

A statement block (also called a **code block**) is a sequence of one or more statements enclosed in curly braces. This can be included as an element in other compound statements. Note that in this case, the block is *not* terminated by a semicolon.

Literals

One of the most important parts of almost any program are specific values such as numbers. These values are called literals. Some literals from the examples above include `10`, `3.50`, and `"Invalid number!"`

Each literal has a specific **data type**. JavaScript supports three **primitive data types**: numbers, strings, and booleans.

Numbers are written as a sequence of digits, with or without a decimal point. Minus signs are included for negative numbers. Unlike most languages, JavaScript makes no distinction between integers and real (or "floating point") numbers. The following are all valid number literals:

```
523-75    3.1416
```

Internally, JavaScript handles all numbers in floating point form.

Number literals can also be written in exponential form, suitable for very large or small numbers:

`12.8e6` (equivalent to 12800000)

`3.7e-5` (equivalent to 0.000037)

Strings are sequences of text enclosed by either double quotes or single quotes. The type of quotes must be the same at each end. For example:

```
'Hello there!'
"Invalid number!"
'The answer is "yes"'
""
```

Strings enclosed by double quotes may contain single quotes, and vice versa. A string with no characters is the **empty string** or **null string**.

Finally, **boolean** literals consist of one of the words: `true` or `false`. These literals mean exactly what they say. Notice that these are words, not strings, and they are composed entirely of lower-case letters.

If a calculation or input that should produce a number results in an invalid number, the result is given the special value **NaN** (Not-a-Number). This is a number literal, not a string!

JavaScript actually supports five primitive datatypes, not three. The others are **undefined** and **null**. Values of these types sometimes indicate that an error has occurred, but they are handled just as though they are normal values.

Identifiers

Another important element of a JavaScript program is **identifiers**. These provide names for things like variables and functions, which we will see soon. Like any language, JavaScript has some simple rules for the form of identifiers:

1. Identifiers may consist only of letters, digits, and the special characters '$' (dollar sign) and '_' (underscore).
2. Identifiers may not begin with a digit.

Identifiers can be as simple as single letters like `x` and `y`, but it is a good idea to make them a little longer and more meaningful. There is no fixed limit on length, but of course extremely long identifiers are hard to work with.

Note that JavaScript identifiers are case sensitive. The names `Price`, `price`, and `PRICE` are all distinct.

There is also a list of names called **reserved words** that cannot be used as identifiers because they have a special use in the language. For example, you cannot use `var` or `else` as identifiers. A complete list is given in Appendix A.

In addition to these rules, most JavaScript programmers follow the *convention* that identifiers composed of multiple words should be written in **camel case**. This means that the words should be directly adjoined, and that all except the first should start with an upper-case letter. The name of a variable representing an ice cream flavor would be written `iceCreamFlavor`. This is an example of a preferred programming style.

Functions

Even the simplest program requires the use of some statements that are packaged as subprograms, not fully written into the program itself. The JavaScript interpreter provides a library of "built-in" subprograms. In addition, programmers write their own subprograms to provide a manageable organization to their complete program.

JavaScript subprograms are called **functions**. A function is a block of code which is created to perform a particular task. Some functions are designed to calculate and return a value, while others simply perform a sequence of statements related to the same task. In the program above, for example, prompt is a function. This function is called by the statement:

```
var innum = prompt("Type a number between 1 and 10");
```

The `prompt` function performs a series of steps, described in the next section. It is highly impractical to write all of the detailed statements to accomplish this, every time we need it.

The general format for a function call is:

```
function name ( argument 1 , ... , argument n);
```

The **arguments** are a set of values to be assigned to the various **parameters** that have been defined for this particular function. The function call is a type of expression; it produces a value which is typically then used in an assignment statement. You will learn a lot more about functions, including how to write your own, in a future chapter.

A JavaScript function is also called a **method**, and methods are associated with **objects**. In this example, `prompt` is a method of the object `window`, and `write` is a method of the object `document`. You will learn more later about objects and their methods. We will also see why `document` is written in the program, and `window` is not.

Don't worry if functions, arguments, and parameters are confusing at first. We'll go over it in much more detail in a later chapter.

Comments

There are two lines in our example program that have not yet been discussed. These are:

```
// Get an input number

// If valid, display its square
```

These lines are **comments**. They provide some explanation of what is being done. Any line that starts with `//` (two slashes) is ignored by the JavaScript interpreter and is considered to be a comment.

Comments are very important. Even when your code is very brief and simple, it is likely that someone will need to read and understand it in the future. Without comments it is much more likely that future readers will not fully understand the purpose of each statement.

It is also possible to place a comment after a statement on the same line. If two slashes appear after the semicolon that ends a statement, the rest of the line is considered to be a comment. Single line comments always begin with two slashes and finish at the end of the current line. Here is an example:

```
var days = 0;  // Number of days until Friday
```

Another type of comment can span multiple lines, perhaps to give a more extended explanation of what is being done in a larger section of code. A line that begins with `/*` (A slash followed by an asterisk) introduces a comment that does not end until the closing sequence `*/` is encountered. At the beginning of our example program, we might write:

```
/*
    This program accepts an input from 1 to 10
```

```
                and calculates its square
    */
```

Input and Output

A program can only be useful if it has some effect on its environment, which represents the program output. Most commonly this means displaying some results on a computer screen or mobile device. Output could also include various types of audio, turning a light on or off, controlling an automobile, or manipulating objects on a web page.

The primary purpose of JavaScript is to interact with web pages, so its effect is most often seen indirectly by updating a web display. But it is certainly possible to have a JavaScript program produce a simple text display as output, as we have done in our first demonstration programs. The following line:

```
        document.write('Welcome to JavaScript!');
```

shows one way to produce simple text output. This will display a line of text, but it will delete any content that was there before. If the statement executes after the page has finished loading, it will erase anything already on the page. This is usually not what we want, but it is good enough for some simple examples. You will learn better ways to produce output very soon.

Some type of input is also needed by most programs. For JavaScript, this may often consist of user actions like pressing buttons, but it may also be necessary to receive and respond to text input. This can be difficult because there can be many ways to input the same information. How many ways can you think of for typing today's date?

In this chapter we have used the following function (or method) to obtain input:

```
    var inputNum = prompt("type a number between 1 and 10");
```

The `prompt` method displays a pop-up window containing the given text as a prompt. The user can type some text which is returned as a string. The string is usually saved using an assignment statement. It is up to the rest of the program to validate the string and make use of it.

21

Again, this is not the only way or even the best way to obtain input, but we will use it in our examples for now. Other types of input will be discussed when we need them.

Now we know enough to get started with the technical details of constructing a JavaScript program. In the next chapter we can begin to write programs that really do something.

Chapter 4: Computing Results

The basic purpose of a computer, since its earliest days, has been to do calculations and compute results. Thus, it is not surprising that one of the primary tasks of most JavaScript programs, or programs in any language, is to perform computations. To see how this works, we need several more program elements.

Variables

We know we can express values, at least of the three basic data types, as literals. These values are very useful, but once written into a program their value will never change. A literal value of 3.5 will always be 3.5.

A **variable** may be thought of as a container that holds a value. Values in a variable can be changed by program statements. A variable named `cost` can begin with a value of 10 and later be given another value such as 25 or 12.3.

Variables have names and these names must follow the rules for identifiers as discussed in Chapter 3.

A variable also has a data type that is the data type of its current value. In many languages, the data type of a variable is fixed and cannot change. In JavaScript, a variable can be set to a value of any type and takes on the data type of that value.

You can create as many variables as you like, as long as each one has a distinct name that conforms to the rules for identifiers. A variable is created by declaring it using the keyword `var`:

```
var x;
var cost;
var numberOfTrees;
```

Once a variable is created, it should be given a value. The most common way to do this will be considered next.

Newer versions of JavaScript define two additional ways to declare variables, using the keywords `let` and `const`. These will be explained in a later chapter.

Assignment Statements

The most common way to store a value in a variable is to use an assignment statement. This statement, which we mentioned before, is at the heart of almost any program. At its very simplest, an assignment statement looks like:

```
variable = value;
```

For example:

```
cost = 13.75;
numberOfTrees = 300;
```

The effect of these statements is to *assign* the value on the right to the variable on the left. This should not be confused with stating an equality, even though the familiar equals sign (=) is used. We are not *stating* that `cost` and 13.75 are equal; we are *making* them equal by placing the value 13.75 into the variable `cost`.

These statements assume that the variables named in the assignment have already been declared. If you assign a value to a variable that has not been declared, you may get unexpected results.

If this is the first assignment to a particular variable, you can declare it and assign it a value at the same time:

```
var cost = 13.75;
```

In the examples so far, the value for the assignment has been given by a literal. This value, of course, may also be another variable:

```
numberOfTrees = treeCount;
```

We must assume here that `treeCount` has a value, perhaps set by a previous assignment statement. This is a good assumption because JavaScript makes sure all variables *always* have a value. When a variable is declared, if it is not immediately assigned a value, JavaScript gives it the special value **undefined**. This may not seem too useful, but it does avoid an actual error if the variable is used before a real value is assigned to it.

The usefulness of the assignment statement would be limited if we could only assign individual values. We would like instead to be able to write statements like:

```
numberOfTrees = treeCount - deadTreeCount;
totalCost = costPerItem * numberOfItems;
```

For this reason, we really need the assignment statement to have the more general form:

```
variable = expression;
```

Here an expression may be a single value, or it may be a collection of values grouped into terms and connected by various operators. This sounds a lot like the familiar idea of an arithmetic expression. While this is one type of expression you can use, the assignment statement may contain other types of expressions as well. We will consider operators and expressions in the next section.

There is one more thing to realize about assignments. Because an assignment is an action, not a declaration of equality, it is perfectly reasonable to have the same variable on the right and left sides of the assignment. We can write:

```
price = price - discount;
```

This statement computes a value based on the original `price`, then stores that value as the new `price`.

Operators and Expressions

Expressions in JavaScript represent values. Most arithmetic expressions that you are familiar with are valid JavaScript expressions, as long as they are written in accordance with JavaScript syntax. There are also other types of expressions in JavaScript, which will be less familiar outside of programming.

Operators accept one or more **operands** to produce a new value. An operand may be a literal, a variable, or other expression. Here you will meet many of the most commonly used operators in JavaScript. The operators we will consider are either binary operators (which take two operands), or unary operators (which take only one).

Arithmetic Operators

The most familiar operators are those that perform standard arithmetic on numbers. The following binary operators compute a value from two numbers:

Operator	Purpose	Example
+	add	`cost + profit`
−	subtract	`totalTrees - deadTrees`
*	multiply	`quantity * costEach`
/	divide	`pizzaCost / 3`

The result of applying add, subtract, or multiply is self-evident. Division requires a special note. In many languages, dividing two integers results in an integer, and any remainder is thrown away. For example, 12 / 5 equals 2. In JavaScript, since integers and non-integers are treated equally, the result of dividing two integers may be a non-integer. In JavaScript, 12 / 5 equals 2.4.

The remaining operators may be less familiar. The **modulus** or **remainder** operator gives the remainder from a division operation:

```
x = 25 % 7; // sets x to 4
x = 8.4 % 2.3; // sets x to 1.5
```

The **exponentiation** operator raises the first number to the power of the second number:

```
x = 5 ** 3; // set x to 125 (5 * 5 * 5)
```

Although common in most languages, the exponentiation operator was only added to JavaScript in the ES6 version. It may not be supported by all browsers.

JavaScript also provides several unary number operators. These change the value of a single number. The first two are straightforward:

Operator	Purpose	Effect
+	plus	None. It is redundant

–	minus	Negates the value

The plus operator is a convenience, but it has no effect on the value. The minus operator changes a positive value to a negative one, or a negative value to a positive one.

The next two operators require special attention. Not only do they produce a value, but they also change one of the operands. What's more, the value produced depends on the order in which these two steps are performed!

Operator	Purpose	Examples
++	increment (add 1)	`count++`, `++count`
--	decrement (subtract 1)	`quantity--`, `--quantity`

Ideally, an expression should have no effect but to produce a value. We say an expression containing an increment or decrement operator produces a **side effect** because it also changes one of the operands.

Suppose that `count` has the value 5. Then, the following assignment statement:

```
total = count++;
```

sets `total` to the value of `count`, and *then* adds 1 to `count`. After this assignment, the value of `total` is 5, and the value of `count` is 6. This is a **postfix** operator. It comes *after* the operand and changes the operand *after* using its value.

On the other hand, the statement:

```
total = ++count;
```

first increments `count`, then sets `total` to the *new* value of `count`. After this assignment, the value of `total` is 6, and the value of `count` is 6. This is a **prefix** operator. It comes *before* the operand and changes the operand *before* using its value.

The increment and decrement operators may only be applied to variables. Clearly an expression like $5++$ would not make sense.

In the previous chapter, we introduced the value NaN to represent an invalid number. If *any* of the values in an expression evaluate to NaN, then the value of the entire expression is NaN!

Comparison and Boolean Operators

A large group of binary operators compare two values, giving a boolean (or logical) value as a result. In JavaScript, these are called **comparison** operators, and they are also often known as **relational** operators. In the simplest case, the values compared are both numbers.

Operator	Purpose	Example
==	equal	`cost == 3.5`
!=	not equal	`quantity != 0`
>	greater than	`treeCount > 100`
<	less than	`deadTreeCount < 10`
>=	greater than or equal	`score >= 50`
<=	less than or equal	`count <= 25`

Two binary operators accept two boolean operands and produce a boolean result:

Operator	Purpose	Effect
&&	and	returns `true` if both operands are true
||	or	returns `true` if either operand is true

Finally, a single unary operator reverses the value of a boolean operand:

Operator	Purpose	Effect
!	not	returns `true` if the operand is false

String Operator

The addition operator (+) may be applied to strings. In this case, it performs **concatenation**. If we have two separate strings:

```
var string1 = "Welcome"
var string2 = "to JavaScript"
```

then the expression `string1 + string2` will have the value:

```
"Welcometo JavaScript"
```

Note that this may not be exactly what you want, since there is no space between `"Welcome"` and `"to"`. If you want a space, you need to include it at the end of `string1` or the beginning of `string2`, or add it to the expression like this:

```
string1 + " " + string2
```

Numbers in Strings

JavaScript input is usually in the form of strings, so it is very common to have a string that represents a number, such as `"2500"` or `"31.5"`. If a string like this is used in an arithmetic expression, JavaScript will usually try to treat it like the number it represents:

```
oldWeight = "100";
newWeight = oldWeight * 3;    // newWeight will be 300
newWeight = oldWeight / 4;    // newWeight will be 25
newWeight = oldWeight - 20;   // newWeight will be 80
```

In each of these examples, `newWeight` is assigned a number. However, there is a strange and important exception. Since the plus sign represents string concatenation, if an expression tries to "add" a number string and a number, the number will be changed to a string!

```
newWeight = oldWeight + 20; //newWeight will be "10020"
```

To avoid this unintended result, we need JavaScript to treat `oldWeight` as a number. This can be done by calling the function `Number`, which converts a string to a number. Changing the data type of a value in this way is called **casting**.

```
newWeight = Number(oldWeight) + 20; //newWeight will be 120
```

Assignment Operators

Assignment, represented by the symbol (=), may also be considered an operator. After the expression on the right of the assignment symbol is evaluated, it is assigned to the variable on the left.

This may sound a bit trivial and uninteresting, but assignment statements can be combined with various operators. Remember the example of assignment statements with the same variable on both sides of the assignment symbol? We can write:

```
price = price - discount;
```
But JavaScript also offers a shorter way to write the same thing:

```
price -= discount;
```

The following assignment operators are available to combine an assignment with arithmetic operations:

Operator	Meaning
+=	add and assign
-=	subtract and assign
*=	multiply and assign
/=	divide and assign

While JavaScript provides several kinds of shorthand notation like these assignment operators, it may not always be a good idea to use them. It is usually more important to write code that others can read and understand, rather than making every statement as short as possible!

Grouping and Precedence

The JavaScript operators that we have seen use at most two operands at a time, but expressions may include many operators and operands. For example, we may write:

```
price = cost + profit - discount;
totalCost = downPayment + monthlyCost *
```

30

```
                    numberOfMonths;
```
or even
```
okToProceed = mainFuel + extraFuel >= 20 &&
              windSpeed < 10;
```

In these cases, rules are needed to determine the order in which the operators are applied. This is the problem of **operator precedence**. In many cases, this is determined the same way it would be in basic arithmetic, with two primary rules:

1. Evaluation proceeds left to right
2. Multiplication and division are performed before addition and subtraction

These rules are often all we need. In the first example, we add `cost` to `profit`, then subtract `discount` from the sum. In the second example, multiplication is performed first, followed by addition.

The third example is less obvious since the expression includes both comparison and logical operators. JavaScript expressions often combine datatypes, and there are precedence rules for all operators. In particular, arithmetic operators have a higher precedence than comparison operators, and comparison operators have a higher precedence than boolean operators.

Here is a table of precedence for the operators we have seen so far, from highest at the top to lowest at the bottom:

`++, -- (postfix)`
`++, -- (prefix),!`
`**`
`*, /, %`
`+, -`
`<, <=, >, >=`
`==, !=`
`&&, ||`
`=, +=, -=, *=, /=`

Note that some of these are less obvious than others.

For operators with the same level of precedence, the left-to-right rule is followed. Suppose this is not what you want. The well-known solution to changing the precedence is to enclose a subexpression in parentheses. Expressions in parentheses are always evaluated first before their value is used outside the parentheses. If we write:

```
cost = (cost + surcharge) * discount;
```

The addition will be done first. We can say that parentheses are an operator, with higher precedence than any other operator on the list.

Chapter 5: Making Choices

The JavaScript features we have seen so far allow us to declare variables, to assign them values based on expressions, and to do simple input and output. These features are important, but very few programs will be composed of just a series of assignments all in a fixed sequence. We need to be able to change the sequence based on a variety of conditions. For this, we need conditional statements.

Conditions

A conditional statement takes actions depending on conditions. A condition is an expression with a boolean value. Conditions must evaluate to either `true` or `false`.

Conditions in conditional statements are always enclosed in parentheses. A condition could be a simple boolean variable:

```
(loggedIn)
```

or a more complex expression:

```
(age >= 21 && hour >= 9 && day != "Sunday")
```

These expressions primarily make use of the comparison and boolean operators discussed in the previous chapter.

If Statement

You have already met the **if statement** briefly at the start of Chapter 3. This statement allows you to execute a statement or a group of statements only if a given condition is true. In the simplest case, it has the form:

`if` (*condition*) {*statement block*}

The condition is a boolean expression that must evaluate to be either `true` or `false`. The statement block is a sequence of zero or more statements (yes, it can be zero) enclosed in curly braces. If the condition is true, the statements in the block are executed. If the condition is false, nothing happens.

For example, we can write:

```
if (snowDepth > 4) {
    thermostatSetting = 70;
    getShovel = true;
}
```

Note that by the usual style conventions, the curly braces for a statement block are on different lines than the statements. This is recommended, but not necessary.

If there is only one statement, the braces are optional. However, it is a good idea to include them in all cases to ensure code readability.

If-Else Statement

In many cases, we want to execute one set of statements if the given condition is `true`, and another set if it is `false`. We can extend the **if** statement to the **if-else** statement:

`if` (*condition*) {*statement block 1*} `else` {*statement block 2*}

If the condition evaluates to `true`, statement block 1 is executed. If the condition evaluates to `false`, statement block 2 is executed. In either case, the program continues with the next statement. We can write:

```
if (snowDepth > 4) {
    ethermostatSetting = 70;
    getShovel = true;
} else {
    thermostatSetting = 65;
    getShovel = false;
}
```

It is also common that there are more than two choices. For example, a movie ticket may have several different prices, depending on whether the ticket is for a child, a senior, or a younger adult. In this situation, we can use the **else-if** statement:

```
if (age < 12) {
    ticketPrice = 5.00;
} else if (age > 60) {
```

34

```
        ticketPrice = 7.50;
    } else {
        ticketPrice = 10.00;
    }
```

Of course, the ticket agent has to decide how to determine the patron's age!

Switch Statement

The if, if-else, and else-if statements can handle almost all situations where the program action is dependent on some conditions. However, JavaScript provides alternate syntax for the very common case where the action is determined by the value of an expression.

The **switch statement** consists of the keyword switch followed by an expression and a sequence of **case clauses** enclosed in curly braces. Each case clause in turn consists of the keyword case followed by an expression, a colon (:), and a sequence of statements (*not* enclosed in curly braces). The structure is:

switch (*expression*) { *case clause ... case clause* }

where each case clause is:

case *expression* : *sequence of statements*

The **switch** statement is especially useful if there are a large number of cases. Suppose that stateCode contains a number from 1 to 6 representing one of the New England United States. The following code could be used to set stateName to the name of the state:

```
var stateName;
switch (stateCode) {
    case 1:
        stateName = "Maine";
        break;
    case 2:
        stateName = "New Hampshire";
        break;
    case 3:
        stateName = "Vermont";
        break;
    case 4:
```

```
            stateName = "Massachusetts";
            break;
        case 5:
            stateName = "Connecticut";
            break;
        case 6:
            stateName = "Rhode Island";
    }
```

The **switch** statement compares the value of the expression with the value given by each **case** clause. If the values match, the following statements up to the next **case** clause are executed.

What is the purpose of the **break** statement in the example? The break statement indicates that the flow of control should exit the block in which it occurs. In this case, the break statement will cause the next statement after the switch block to execute.

By default, once a case has been matched, the statements in *all following case clauses* are executed until the keyword `break` is encountered. It does not even matter if the cases in the remaining clauses are matched!

This is not often what is wanted, and this is where the **break** statement comes in. The purpose of this statement is to exit the **switch** statement and continue with the code that follows. If we were to write:

```
switch (stateCode) {
    case 1:
        stateName = "Maine";
    case 2:
        stateName = "New Hampshire";
    case 3:
        stateName = "Vermont";
    case 4:
        stateName = "Massachusetts";
    case 5:
        stateName = "Connecticut";
    case 6:
        stateName = "Rhode Island";
}
```

then for any value of `stateCode` from 1 to 6, `stateName` would always be set to `"Rhode Island"`. By placing a **break** statement at the end of each clause, we ensure that once a match occurs, only one statement group will be executed. For the last case, the break is optional, since the statement is at the end anyway.

What if the value in `stateCode` is not an integer between 1 and 6? In this case, none of the cases will match, and `stateName` will have the value **undefined**. To ensure that this variable always has a value, we can add a **default clause** at the end of all the case clauses:

```
var stateName;
switch (stateCode) {
    case 1:
        stateName = "Maine";
        break;
    case 2:
        stateName = "New Hampshire";
        break;
    case 3:
        stateName = "Vermont";
        break;
    case 4:
        stateName = "Massachusetts";
        break;
    case 5:
        stateName = "Connecticut";
        break;
    case 6:
        stateName = "Rhode Island";
        break;
    default:
        stateName = "invalid state";
}
```

The statements in the default clause will be executed if none of the cases provide a match.

The syntax of the switch statement is a little unusual. Note the following:

- The value given in the **case** clause can be an expression, but it is not enclosed in parentheses.
- The sequence of statements after each case is a statement block, but it is not enclosed in curly braces.

More About Conditions

We have seen that a string consisting of a number, such as "25", may sometimes be treated as a number in expressions. For example:

```
x = 500;
y = x - "25";
```

results in storing the number 475 in variable `y`.

Does JavaScript consider such a string and the number it contains to be completely equal? That is, does the expression `25 == "25"` have the value `true`?

The answer is yes! The operator (`==`) tests the equality of values, not data types, and may convert a string to a number before comparing. However, JavaScript provides another comparison operator we haven't previously mentioned, composed of *three* equals signs (`===`). This is the **strictly equal** operator. The expression `a === b` will be true only if `a` and `b` have the same value *and* the same type. So, `25 === "25"` has the value `false`.

This is relevant to switch statements because the switch statement makes an implicit comparison between the switch expression and each case expression, and this comparison is based on strict equality. If the switch expression evaluates to "25" and the case expression evaluates to 25, the case clause will not be executed.

Beginning with ES5, JavaScript has an option known as **strict mode**. If a function or an entire script begins with the line:

```
'use strict';
```

then the interpreter will use a much stricter set of syntax rules that will cause errors if they are not followed precisely. Strict mode is complex, and we will not discuss it further in this book.

JavaScript provides another short form for the situation where the value to be assigned to a variable depends on a condition. For this we would normally write:

```
if (age < 8) {
    mealPrice = 1.00;
} else {
    mealPrice = 5.00;
}
```

We can write this more compactly using the **conditional assignment** operator (?). This is a **ternary** operator; it uses three different values to compute a result:

```
mealPrice = (age < 8) ? 1.00 : 5.00;
```

Repetition

The examples in this chapter have used conditions to determine whether certain statements should be executed. After these statements, whether executed or not, the program continues to the next statements that follow the condition.

Another very important use of conditions is to control the repetition of statements. A conditional statement may be used to repeat a statement block as long as a particular condition is `true`. We will consider this type of statement in the next chapter.

Chapter 6: Repeating Yourself

Adding conditional statements like **if** and **switch** to your programs is an important step forward. These statements take an action based on a condition, then proceed forward in a straight line. There are many times, though, when you may wish to repeat a sequence of statements more than once, as long as a certain condition is `true`. We consider these statements in this chapter.

While Statement

The **while** statement, or **while loop**, specifies that a statement block is to be executed repeatedly as long as a given condition is `true`. If the condition is `false` at the start, the statements are never executed. The statement has the form:

```
while (condition) { sequence of statements }
```

For example, suppose you want to add up a series of numbers that a user may type, stopping when a zero is typed. You could write:

```
var total = 0;
var input = prompt("Enter a number, or 0 to stop");
while (input != 0) {
    total += Number(input);
    input = prompt("Enter a number, or 0 to stop");
}
document.write("Total equals " + total);
```

This program prompts for a number, then adds that number to the variable total, unless the number is 0. Due to the **while** loop, the actions are repeated until a value of 0 is seen. Then the program exits and displays the total. Each repetition is called an **iteration**.

If the condition in a while loop does not depend on input, it must depend on something that changes during the statement block, that will eventually make the condition `true`. Otherwise, the loop will repeat forever. This is called an infinite loop and will cause the user's browser to freeze and probably crash.

This program illustrates the **while** loop, but we have also slipped in several other details that you have not previously seen:

- To compute a sum one value at a time, we declare a variable (`total`) and initialize it to zero. We can then add the new input value on each iteration of the loop.

- The first `prompt` statement must come before the `while` to obtain the first value to be tested. The remaining prompts must come at the end of the loop statement. We will see how the variation in the next section avoids this problem.

- The input obtained from the prompt statement is a string. If we write:

```
total += input;
```

which as you know is equivalent to:

```
total = total + input;
```

we are adding a number to a string. As you remember from Chapter 4, in this case the symbol (+) will be taken as concatenation, and the number will be converted to a string.

To solve this last problem, we use the built-in function `Number`. This function converts a string containing a number literal to an actual number.

Run this program, inputting several numerical values followed by zero. Then run it again, giving a non-number input such as "`abc`". Finally, remove the `Number` function, and run the program one more time to see what happens.

Do While Statement

The **while** statement tests a condition *before* executing its statement block. If the condition is `false`, the statement block is never executed.

The similarly named **do while** statement tests a condition **after** executing its statement block. With this statement, the statement block will **always** run at least once.

The format for the `do while` statement is:

```
do { sequence of statements } while (condition);
```

Note that unlike the **while** statement, the **do while** should end with a semicolon. Like other statements in JavaScript, it is considered good practice to include the semicolon after a **do while** loop. However, omitting it will not generate an error.

Our previous program can be changed to use the **do while** statement:

```
var total = 0;
do {
    input = prompt("Enter a number, or 0 to stop");
    total += Number(input);
} while (input != 0);
document.write("Total equals " + total);
```

This is a little simpler than the previous program because the prompt statement does not have to be written twice. The drawback is that the statements in the loop will always run at least once, even if the first input is zero. Fortunately, in this specific example, that makes no difference. What has changed in the code to accommodate this requirement?

In many languages, the **do while** is replaced by a **do until**, and the condition is reversed.

For Statement

The **while** statement (along with the **do while**) may be all we really need to implement conditional loops, but JavaScript, like most languages, provides a special statement to simplify the program code for a common and important case.

Very often you may need to perform some action a specific number of times. For example, suppose you want to display a table of the first ten factorials. (Hint: In mathematics, the factorial of an integer is the product of all positive integers less than or equal to itself. For example, 4! is equal to 4 * 3 * 2 * 1, or 24.) Consider the following example:

```
var val = 1;
var count = 1;
var fact = 1;
document.write ("<pre>VALUE      FACTORIAL\n");
while (count <= 10) {
    document.write (val + "              " + fact + "\n");
    count++;
    val++;
    fact = fact * val;
}
document.write ("</pre>");
```

First, note that the output from `document.write` and other JavaScript output methods must actually be HTML code to be displayed by the browser. This has not mattered in our previous examples, but this example has more structure.

In this code, we have used the HTML tags `<pre>` ... `</pre>` to indicate that the enclosed output should be considered preformatted. The only other thing to note right now is that the string "`\n`" is a special code that generates a new line.

One useful simplification we have used: since we know the loop is to be executed at least once (in fact more than once) the main output line does not have to be repeated. We could have used the **do while** as well:

```
var val = 1;
var count = 1;
var fact = 1;
document.write ("<pre>VALUE      FACTORIAL\n");
do {
     document.write ( val + "                " + fact + "\n");
     count++;
     val++;
     fact = fact * val;
} while (count <= 10);
document.write ("</pre>");
```

This program will work, but since we are repeating a fixed number of times, there is a simpler form that we can use based on the **for** statement:

```
var val = 1;
var fact = 1;
document.write ("<pre>VALUE      FACTORIAL\n");
for (var count = 1; count <= 10; count++) {
     document.write ( val + "              " + fact + "\n");
     fact = fact * ++val;
}
document.write ("</pre>");
```

The **for** statement can simplify three important steps that are generally needed when repeating a loop a fixed number of times:

1. initializing the **count variable**
2. testing the **termination condition**
3. updating the count variable

The general format is:

```
for (statement 1 ; statement 2 ; statement 3 )
    {sequence of statements}
```

A **count variable** is generally needed to count the iterations. This variable is then compared to a limit value in the termination condition. The usual purpose of statement 1 is to initialize the count variable. This statement is executed once at the beginning of the loop. Note that this variable, like all variables, should be declared with the keyword `var`, either within statement 1 or at some previous point in the program. If you skip this step, you won't generate an error in your code. However, it could result in unintended consequences related to variable scope, which will be discussed in a later chapter.

Statement 2 usually represents the termination condition. This condition is evaluated at the beginning of each iteration. If its value is false, the loop terminates.

Statement 3 is generally used to update the count variable. Often this means to increment or decrement it by 1.

Although this discussion describes the usual and intended purpose of these three statements, JavaScript will allow them to be almost anything, including empty statements. However, your code may be difficult to understand, and likely to contain errors, if you get too clever in your use of these statements!

Many JavaScript objects represent sets of variables or values. When you learn about these objects, you will also learn some new variations on the **for** statement.

Break and Continue

You have met the **break** statement, which was used to exit a **switch** statement unconditionally when the appropriate case clause had been executed. The `break` statement may be used within the statement block of any of the loop statements discussed here. For example, we may want to extend the table of factorials, but stop if the value gets too high:

```
var val = 1;
var fact = 1;
document.write ("<pre>VALUE      FACTORIAL\n");
for (var count = 1; count <= 100; count++) {
    document.write ( val + "            " + fact + "\n");
    fact = fact * ++val;
    if (fact > 999999999999999) break;
}
document.write ("</pre>");
```

This example will stop generating the table when the factorial value would exceed 15 decimal digits, which occurs for values greater than 17 factorials. JavaScript is required to correctly handle integers at least this large.

The **continue** statement is only used with loops. It is best used with **for loops**, but technically you could use it with a **while** or a **do while** loop. However, it is very easy to create an infinite loop if the `continue` statement executes before the control variable is incremented. The `continue` statement tells the program to quit the current iteration of the loop but continue with the next one. This version of the previous program will skip the output for values that are multiples of three:

```
var val = 1;
var fact = 1;
document.write ("<pre>VALUE      FACTORIAL\n");
for (var count = 1; count <= 100; count++) {
    if (val % 3 == 0) {
        fact *= ++val;
        continue;
    }
    document.write ( val + "              " + fact + "\n");
    fact *= ++val;
    if (fact > 999999999999999) break;
}
document.write ("</pre>");
```

It is also possible to place a label on a statement and have the `break` or `continue` statements transfer execution to that label. This is useful when the `break` or `continue` is nested inside two or more loop or conditional structures.

For example, suppose in the `switch` example from the previous chapter, we want the user to type a state name, print the state code, repeat 5 times, but quit if the user types "stop". We might try the following program:

```
var stateCode, stateName;
document.write("<pre>");
for (var count = 1; count <= 5; count++) {
    stateName =
        prompt('Type a state name, or "stop" to quit');

    switch (stateName) {
        case "Maine":
            stateCode = 1;
            break;
        case "New Hampshire":
            stateCode = 2;
```

```
                    break;
          case "Vermont":
                    stateCode = 3;
                    break;
          case "Massachusetts":
                    stateCode = 4;
                    break;
          case "Connecticut":
                    stateCode = 5;
                    break;
          case "Rhode Island":
                    stateCode = 6;
          case "stop":
                    stateCode = 0;
                    break;
          default:
                    stateCode = 0;
     }

     if (stateCode > 0) {
          document.write("State code is "
                    + stateCode + "\n");
     } else {
          document.write("Invalid state code!\n");
     }
}
document.write("Program done\n</pre>");
```

This may be close to what we want, but it will not actually work. If "stop" is typed, the program will recognize it as an invalid state name, but it will still continue with the next repetition.

One solution is to replace the for statement with a more complicated while statement, which counts the iterations, but also checks for the string "stop". However, another solution is to use a **labelled break statement**:

```
var stateCode, stateName;
document.write("<pre>");
stateLoop: for (var count = 1; count <= 5; count++) {
     stateName =
          prompt('Type a state name, or "stop" to quit');

     switch (stateName) {
          case "Maine":
                    stateCode = 1;
                    break;
```

```
        case "New Hampshire":
            stateCode = 2;
            break;
        case "Vermont":
            stateCode = 3;
            break;
        case "Massachusetts":
            stateCode = 4;
            break;
        case "Connecticut":
            stateCode = 5;
            break;
        case "Rhode Island":
            stateCode = 6;
        case "stop":
            break stateLoop;
        default:
            stateCode = 0;
    }
    if (stateCode > 0) {
        document.write("State code is " + stateCode);
    } else {
        document.write("Invalid state name!\n");
    }
}
document.write("Program done\n</pre>");
```

With this method, a label is placed on the enclosing loop, and the `break` statement refers to the loop label to indicate that its purpose is to exit completely from the enclosing loop. Without the label, the break could only exit from the switch statement.

Labels may only be placed on loop statements (`while`, `do while`, or `for`) or on a statement block. A `break` statement that refers to such a label may only appear inside the block to signal an exit from the entire block.

Many early languages allowed labels on *any* statement and provided a **goto statement** to transfer to any label from almost anywhere in the program. This is now considered a bad way to write programs and is not included in modern languages.

As noted at the start of this section, a `continue` statement may also refer to a label under some conditions. This is useful primarily when a loop is nested inside another loop. This will be discussed further in Chapter 10.

Chapter 7: Input, Output, and the DOM

Up to now we have performed very simple input and output using the `prompt` and `document.write` functions. This works but it is not very useful. The `prompt` function creates a small pop-up in the middle of the browser window, with a box where text can be typed. The `document.write` function displays one or more lines of output, but only after deleting everything that was previously present in the window. For general input and output, though, we need a more robust method.

The Document Object Model

To achieve more flexible input and output of text in the context of a web page, we can make use of the HTML **Document Object Model (DOM)**. This model represents any web page in such a way that individual elements on the page can be referred to, examined and modified, by program statements in a language such as JavaScript. We will look briefly at the DOM here and you will learn more about it in Chapter 14.

Consider the simple HTML framework shown below:

```
<!DOCTYPE html>
<html>
<head>
    <title>JavaScript Demo Page</title>
</head>
<body>

    <h1>JavaScript Demo Page</h1>

    <form id="inform">
        Enter a number between 1 and 10:<br>
        <input type="text" id="textin">

    </form>

    <br>
    <button onclick="findSquare(inform)">Run</button>

    <br><br>
    The square of your number is:<br>
    <p id="textout"></p>
    <br>
```

```
<script src=square.js></script>


</body>
</html>
```

There are a few HTML elements in this example we haven't seen before. We will get to these shortly. First, we want to note that this page, like all HTML pages, forms a hierarchy, with various elements enclosed in HTML tags that may in turn enclose other elements.

We can use this HTML code together with a JavaScript file to compute the square of a number as we did in Chapter 3. However, this time both the input value and the output value will appear on the same page. The corresponding JavaScript should be in a file named `square.js`. The content of this file is:

```
function findSquare(formId) {

    // Get the input value
    var inputNum = formId.textin.value;

    // If valid, compute its square
    var result;
    if (inputNum >= 1 && inputNum <= 10) {
        result = inputNum*inputNum;

    // Otherwise, store an error message
    } else {
        result = "Invalid number!";
    }

    // Display the result
    document.getElementById("textout").innerHTML = result;

}
```

The JavaScript file contains a **function definition** for the function `findSquare()`, which is called by the HTML when the button is clicked.

Go ahead and create these two files, place them in the same directory, and run `square.html` in your browser. You should see a page such as:

JavaScript Demo Page

Enter a number between 1 and 10:

Run

The square of your number is:

Enter a valid number in the box and click Run. You should see the answer at the bottom of the page. If you enter anything else, you will get an error message. You can test this example as many times as you like, and you will always stay on the same page.

The DOM allows us to identify elements by specifying their location in the hierarchy. For example, the `input` element within the form can be referred to as `inform.textin`. Since the form id is passed as an argument to the JavaScript function, we use the parameter name `formId` instead of `inform`.

The `input` element is a **void element;** it has attributes but does not have content or an end tag. One attribute of input is `value`, which contains the input string that the user types. To obtain this string, we append the word `value` to the element identifier:

```
var inputNum = formId.textin.value;
```

We can access any element on the page through the hierarchy, but it is often simpler to locate elements by their unique id attribute. For this, we use the function `document.getElementById()`. Again, this function accesses the element itself; to get or set the actual content of an element that is *not* void, we append `innerHTML`.
We can write:

```
value = document.getElementById("textin").value;
```

to obtain the `value` attribute of the `input` element with the id `"textin"`, but we should write:

```
document.getElementById("textout").innerHTML = value;
```

to set the content of the `p` element with the id "`textout`" to a new value. Note that the entire page enclosed in `<html>` tags is referred to as `document`.

Let's look a little more closely at the HTML example:

1. The file starts with the line `<!DOCTYPE html>`. Although not strictly necessary, a DOCTYPE declaration is recommended at the start of all document files to ensure that the contents are interpreted correctly.
2. A complete HTML document has two main parts: The `<head>` and the `<body>`. The `<head>` (which is optional in HTML5 and later versions) contains declarations about the content, including possible `<script>` tags. Here, we have used the `<head>` to specify a title (using the `<title>` tag) for the page. This title will usually appear in a title bar or tab in the browser.
3. The `<form>` tag defines a set of sub-elements such as text areas and buttons that allow the user to input information. In this example the `<input>` tag defines a text box for entering a value.
4. The `<h1>` tag defines a top-level heading. By default, the appearance of this heading is handled by the browser. You can override these defaults in a CSS file.
5. The `<br>` tag ends a line or adds vertical space. The `<br>` element is a void element (has no content), so there is no separate end tag.
6. The `<script>` tag is placed at the *end* of the file, just before the `</body>` tag. This ensures that the script will not run until the page is loaded.

A brief overview of HTML is given in Appendix D. This overview covers the aspects of HTML needed for the examples and exercises in this book.

The JavaScript file contains a single function definition. You have already worked with several built-in functions, and you will learn more about defining your own functions in the near future.

The input value is obtained from the form. This value is a string, but as long as it represents a number literal it will be correctly compared to the test values 1 and 10.

The result to be output is stored in the variable `result`. Note that this may be a number or a string, depending on the value test. Since JavaScript does not assign variables a fixed type, this will not matter.

Finally, the result is displayed in the <p> (paragraph) element at the bottom, using the function `document.getElementById()`.

We have also begun including comments in the JavaScript. It is important to do this consistently in the future to make your code easier to understand.

Making it Pretty

Our demo page is adequate for our needs, but it is kind of boring. There are many ways that it can be more attractive, with and without the need for JavaScript code. One thing we may do is add a little color, which we could do purely with the use of **CSS**, which stands for **Cascading Style Sheets**.

Based on the HTML code provided, a browser has to decide and produce a suitable appearance for every element on the page. Generally, the HTML needs to provide guidance for this, although the final decisions are up to the browser.

Originally HTML included tags and attributes for specifying the appearance of elements, such as:

```
<font size=2 face="Times" color="red">
This text is red</font>
```

More recently, it has been realized that the HTML tags should be limited to describing the purpose of each element, and the appearance or "Style" of each element should be described separately. This has led to the definition of style sheets.

A very simple application of style sheets can be used to add a background color to our demo page, color the run button, and the result. This does not change the JavaScript in any way:

```
<!DOCTYPE html>
<html>
<head>
    <title>JavaScript Demo Page</title>

    <style>
        body {
            background-color: lightblue;
        }
```

```
            button {
                  background-color: lightgreen;
                  color: white;
            }
            p {
                  color: red;
                  font-size: large;
            }
      </style>

</head>
<body>
      <h1>JavaScript Demo Page</h1>

      <form id="inform">
            Enter a number between 1 and 10:<br>
            <input type="text" id="textin">

      </form>

      <br>
      <button onclick="findSquare(inform)">Run</button>

      <br><br>
      The square of your number is:<br>
      <p id="textout"></p>

      <br>
      <script src=square.js></script>


</body>
</html>
```

Here we have added a `<style>` section in the `<head>` section. Each entry in this section consists of a tag type followed by a set of style attributes enclosed in curly brackets. Try running this program (with the same .js file). You should now see something like this:

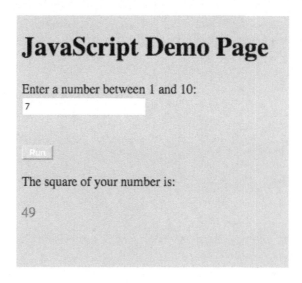

This example will apply the same style to every `<button>` element and every `<p>` element. Fortunately, we have just one of each. But often we have many, and we may want to style individual elements. One way to do this is to give each element a unique id attribute (The `<p>` element already has one, and we can exclude `<body>` since there can only be one of these.). We can then refer to these elements in the `<style>` section by their id preceded by the hash symbol #. We will change the `<button>` tag to the following:

```
<button id="run_button" onclick="findSquare(inform)">
```

and we will revise the `<style>` section as follows:

```
<style>
 body {
      background-color: lightblue;
 }
 #run_button {
      background-color: lightgreen;
      color: white;
 }
 #textout {
      color: red;
      font-size: large;
 }
</style>
```

Try running the code with these revisions. The result should be exactly the same.

The only other thing to note right now is that the style information in the <head> section can get cumbersome and must be repeated for every page. We generally will move this to a separate file. Create a file named square.css with the same content as in the style section, but without the <style> tags:

```
body {
        background-color: lightblue;
}
#run_button {
        background-color: lightgreen;
        color: white;
}
#textout {
        color: red;
        font-size: large;
}
```

To refer to this file, we now place the following line in the <head> section (and remove the former <style> section):

```
<link rel="stylesheet" type="text/css"
        href="square.css">
```

Now save both files and run square.html once more. If we have done this right, the result should still be exactly the same.

This example illustrates a few style attributes. There are many more style attributes in CSS and a variety of ways to refer to individual elements. For more information on this, including why CSS style sheets are called "cascading," see Appendix E.

Another Example

Using this general framework, you can try out most of the examples in this book. For instance, in Chapter 6 we discussed code to generate a table of factorials. Let's put that together with an HTML/CSS framework similar to the previous one.

We will need three files, fact.html, fact,css, and fact.js. The HTML file will be very similar to the previous one:

```
<!DOCTYPE html>
<html>
```

```
<head>
    <title>JavaScript Demo Page</title>
<link rel="stylesheet" type="text/css"
        href="fact.css">
</head>
<body>
    <script src=fact.js></script>

    <h1>JavaScript Demo Page</h1>
    <h2>Factorial table</h2>

    <form id="inform">
        Enter an upper bound for the factorial table:<br>
        <input type="text" id="textin">

    </form>

    <br>
    <button id="run_button"
        onclick="factTable(inform)">Run</button>

    <br><br>
    The factorial table:<br>
    <p id="textout"></p>

    <br>

</body>
```

We have changed a few names, and you may adjust the headings as you like. The introductory sentence is omitted because the JavaScript generates a heading. For this example, we can use exactly the same CSS file, just renamed as `fact.css`.

The JavaScript file is based on the code at the end of Chapter 6.

```
function factTable(formId) {

    // get the limit value
    var limit = formId.textin.value;

    // Make sure limit is a valid number
    if (limit >= 1) {

        // initialize variables
        var val = 1;
        var fact = 1;
        var result = "<pre>VALUE    FACTORIAL\n";


        // generate the table as a string
```

```
        for (var count = 1; count <= limit; count++) {
            result +=  val + "              " + fact + "\n";
            fact = fact * ++val;
            if (fact > 999999999999999) {
                result += "value too large";
                break;
            }
        }
        result += "</pre>";

    } else {
        result = "Invalid limit!";
    }

    // output the table
    document.getElementById("textout").innerHTML = result;
}
```

Manipulating HTML Elements

The above examples provide an effective method for reading conventional text input from a browser and producing text output by using JavaScript. But we can actually go much further. The DOM gives us a method to add, remove, or modify *any* of the elements that may appear on a web page. We'll learn more about this later.

Chapter 8: Functions

Overview

Functions are subprograms that can be called from a JavaScript program to perform an action, and usually return a result. You have seen and used several functions concerned with input and output beginning in Chapters 2 and 3. `document.write` was used to output a line of text. The text was passed as a single string argument.

```
document.write('Welcome to JavaScript!');
```

This function does not provide a return value since the purpose is simply to generate the output.

The second function, `prompt`, was used to input a line of text. The line that was input was returned as a string and stored in a variable:

```
var inputNum = prompt("type a number between 1 and 10");
```

These examples illustrate the general format of a function call:

```
function name (argument 1 , ... , argument n);
```

As we have seen, a function provides a list of **arguments** enclosed in parentheses. Each argument is matched to a **parameter** that is specified in the function definition. If a function has no arguments, the parentheses are still necessary when it is called:

```
x = myFunc();
```

One more function that we have already used in Chapter 7 is:

```
getElementById():
document.getElementById("textout").innerHTML = value;
```

If this statement is a little confusing, it is because we have combined two steps. We could also write:

```
var elem = document.getElementById("textout");
elem.innerHTML = value;
```

Here the first statement gets the element identified by `"textout"` in the object `elem`, and the second statement assigns a value to the `innerHTML` property of `elem`.

Function Definitions

Chapter 7 contains examples of function definitions for the functions `findSquare()` and `factTable()`. The general form is:

```
function name (parameter 1 , ... , parameter n){
     function body
}
```

Each occurrence of a parameter name in the body will be replaced with the corresponding argument given in the call. When `findSquare` is called by `findSquare(inform)` in the HTML file, the function will run with `inform` as its argument. The first line of `findSquare()` then becomes:

```
var inputNum = inform.textin.value;
```

Each of these functions produces an output by modifying an element on the web page without returning a value. Many functions return a value. This is done by a **return statement** such as:

```
return result;
```

This statement does two things:
1. It terminates the function.
2. It provides `result` as the **return value** of the function.

For example, the following function finds the average of 3 values:

```
function avg3 (val1, val2, val3) {
    return (val1 + val2 + val3) / 3;
}
```

A function that returns a value may be used in an expression just like a variable:

```
ans = base + avg3 (x, y, z);
```

It is possible to have a function definition inside another function definition. This is called a **nested function**.

Function Invocation

A function that is defined within an HTML document may be placed anywhere within that document using the `<script>` tag. The function will *not* be executed automatically. It will only be executed under one of two conditions:

1. When it is explicitly called from JavaScript code, such as in the examples above.
2. When a suitable **event** occurs.

Examples of events include loading a page or clicking a button. In Chapter 7, the HTML code in each example defines a button using a line such as:

```
<button onClick="findSquare(inform)">Run</button>
```

This line specifies that the function `findSquare()` should be called with the argument `inform` whenever the button is clicked by the user.

Events are discussed in more detail in Chapter 11.

Anonymous Functions

In JavaScript, in contrast to many other languages, a function may be set as the value of a variable. The function is then invoked using the variable as its "name". These functions have no actual name, so they are referred to as **anonymous functions**.

For example:

```
var a3 = function (val1, val2, val3) {
    return (val1 + val2 + val3) / 3;
}
```

This statement creates an anonymous function to find the average of three arguments and stores the function in the variable a3. The function can then be called by a statement like:

```
var avg = a3 (5, 20, 100);
```

Why would we do this? The answer is that we can do more things with a variable like a3 than with a function name. If JavaScript functions are *first class objects*, they can be used wherever variables can be used. For example, we could write a function that takes a function and three arguments as its own arguments, and applies that function to those arguments:

```
function apply3 (func, val1, val2, val3) {
    return func(val1, val2, val3);
}
```

We can then write the following:

```
var avg = apply3 (a3, 5, 20, 100);
```

to get the same result as we did above. But we might also have a function definition that finds the maximum of three values:

```
var max3 = function (val1, val2, val3) {
    var max = val1;
    if (val2 > max) {
        max = val2;
    }
    if (val3 > max) {
        max = val3;
    }
    return max;
}
```

Then if we write:

```
var avg = apply3 (max3, 5, 20, 100);
```

we will get the maximum instead.

If a function can be assigned to a variable, does this make a function a new data type? The answer is found in the paragraph above. Functions are *first class objects* because functions, like almost everything else in JavaScript, are *objects*. We will say more about this in the next chapter.

Arrow Functions

Once again, JavaScript offers an alternate syntax for some functions that is shorter, but more cryptic. This syntax, called arrow functions, applies to simple anonymous functions.

Using the arrow function syntax, the example given above, which assigns a function that averages three values to variable a3. We could write it as the following:

```
var a3 = (val1, val2, val3) => {
    return (val1 + val2 + val3) / 3;
}
```

Here we have eliminated the keyword `function` and inserted an "arrow" symbol => after the parameter list. This may not seem very useful, but we are not done yet.

If the function has only one statement, and that is a `return` statement, we can eliminate the brackets and the `return` keyword:

```
var a3 = (val1, val2, val3) => (val1 + val2 + val3) / 3;
```

The parentheses around the parameter list are necessary if there are two or more parameters, and also if there are no parameters at all. In the special case of exactly one parameter, the parentheses may be omitted!

Variable Scope

If a JavaScript program is written top to bottom with no functions, any variable declared in the program may be used anywhere within that program. We say these variables have **global scope**.

Once we introduce functions, though, things are different. Variables declared *outside* of any function still have global scope, but it is also possible to declare variables *inside* the function. These variables *cannot* be used outside the function; in fact, they only exist while the function is being executed. They are said to have **local scope**. Consider the following program:

```
function avg3 (val1, val2, val3) {
     var average = (val1 + val2 + val3) / 3;
     return average;
}
var x = 3;
var y = 5;
var z = 7;
ans = avg3 (x,y,z);
document.write(ans + "   " + average);
```

The reference to `average` in the `document.write` statement will cause an error. This variable does not exist outside of the function.

Also note that within the function, the parameters `val1`, `val2`, and `val3` are treated as local variables, just the same as variables that are declared with local scope.

Variables with global scope can be used anywhere, even inside functions. But if a variable declared in a function has the same name as a variable with global scope, the global variable is hidden and only the local variable can be used. For example, consider the following code:

```
var boilTemp = 212;
var freezeTemp = 32;

function findWaterState (waterTemp) {
     var boilTemp = 100;
     if (waterTemp > boilTemp) {
          return "Steam";
     } else if (waterTemp < freezeTemp) {
          return "Ice";
     } else {
          return "Liquid Water";
     }
}
```

If `waterTemp` is equal to 20, it will be compared to the global value `freezeTemp` and the string `"Ice"` will be returned. But if `waterTemp` equals 150, the string `"Steam"` will be returned because the local variable `boilTemp` will be used, not the global variable.

Let and Const

Originally, all variables in JavaScript were declared using the keyword var. ES-2015 introduced two alternate keywords, `let` and `const`.

The big difference is that variables declared with either of these keywords may have **block scope**. That is, they may be declared within a statement block enclosed in curly braces, and such a declaration will have meaning only within that block. For example, in the statements:

```
{
    var a = 5;
    let b = 7;
}
    var first = a;
    var second = b;
```

The assignment to `first` is fine, but the assignment to `second` will cause an error, because `b` does not exist outside the block.

The keyword `const` works the same as `let`, except that variables declared with `const` must be assigned a value when they are declared, and they may not be assigned another value later on within their scope. We may not have:

```
const SQRT2 = 1.414;
SQRT2 = 1.5;
```

A variable defined by `const` in JavaScript is not always a constant in every sense, but this keyword is generally used to define constants with simple datatypes. By convention, such constants are usually given names with all uppercase letters, such as `PI`.

`let` and `const` also differ from `var` when it comes to hoisting, discussed below.

Hoisting

When a JavaScript program is read by an interpreter, it is natural to expect that the interpreter processes statements in the order that they appear. In particular, variables should not be used before they are declared, and functions, it would seem, should not be called before they are defined.

In JavaScript, however, the interpreter can and does peek ahead. We already know that functions may be defined anywhere in the program, including at the very end, and they can still be used wherever they are needed.

The problem comes with the declaration of variables. It is perfectly legal, if a little strange, to write code such as:

```
x = 3;
y = x;
var x;
```

It may seem that this should not work, but it does because JavaScript provides a feature called **hoisting**. Because of this, all variable declarations within a scope are moved to the beginning, so this is processed as though it was written:

```
var x;
x = 3;
y = x;
```

It is important to realize, though, that it is only the declarations of variables that are hoisted, not their initialization or any other assignment of values. If you write:

```
y = x;
var x = 3;
```

The first line will be flagged as an error because x is undefined.

It is legal in JavaScript to use variables before they are declared, but is it a good idea? The answer is almost always no. Best practice is to always define the variables used by a function at the beginning of the function, and to define the variables used globally at the beginning of the program. If this practice is followed, hoisting is unnecessary.

If a variable is defined using `let` or `const`, hoisting does *not* occur. These variables must be declared before they are used in any way.

Chapter 9: Objects and Methods

Objects

We have now introduced most of the basic elements of the JavaScript language, and we have studied a number of examples. Until now, our examples have been based on the traditional programming style, called **procedural programming**. With this style, programs proceed step-by-step, calling subprograms that may call others and so on. Statements are the primary focus, and data structures are generally considered secondary.

The principal alternative to procedural programming is **object-oriented programming**. With this approach, data is viewed as consisting of **objects**. Objects have **properties** (associated values) and **methods** (associated functions). The detailed implementation of objects is hidden from the rest of the program, and objects are only accessed through their properties and their methods. Object-oriented programming has become the dominant approach in modern programming and is supported by almost all widely-used languages.

In "pure" object-oriented programming, object properties are also hidden from direct access. They can be accessed only by special methods called "getters" and "setters".

JavaScript is not a purely object-oriented language, but it has many of the features needed for this type of programming. Most data structures can be viewed as objects, with associated methods and properties.

Additional object-oriented features, including the concept of **classes**, have been added to the most recent JavaScript versions. We will discuss these in Chapter 13.

Objects now join the very short list of JavaScript data types. Primitive types, which have been introduced earlier, include number, string, boolean, undefined and null. *Everything else* is an object. This includes functions, as we already have noted.

It is actually possible to treat the primitive types number, string, and boolean as objects also, but this is not recommended because it is an inefficient use of memory.

One important JavaScript object that we have already seen is the `document` object. This object represents the HTML document that is currently being processed, and provides the methods for accessing the DOM. These methods are called using **dot notation**; we start with the object name and then add the method name, such as `document.getElementById()`.

Another very important object in web programming with JavaScript is the `window` object. This object represents the browser window in which the current page is displayed. This is the **default object,** also called the **global object**, for all JavaScript programs running in a web browser. Its name may be omitted in object references. So the method name `prompt()`, used alone, is short for `window.prompt()`.

Properties

We know that variables in JavaScript (or any other language) have a name and a value. Properties of an object may be thought of as variables, and they are described by **name:value pairs**. For example:

```
var library = {
     name: "Central Library",
     fiction: 1000,
     nonfiction: 500,
     open: true };
```

This code is an **object literal**. It defines an object representing a library, with four properties: its name, the count of fiction and nonfiction books, and a boolean indicating whether the library is open.

There are two different ways to refer to a specific property; you can use dot notation, or you can put the property name as a string in square brackets:

```
library.fiction = 800;
```
or
```
library["fiction"] = 800;
```

Each notation has its advantages, and both are widely used. It is also possible to add new properties to an object, for example:

```
library.address = "123 Main Street";
```

67

Even though the property `address` did not previously exist for this object, this statement will add it.

To remove a property from an object, use the `delete` keyword:

```
delete library.open;
```

This removes the `open` property entirely from the object.

Besides properties such as these that behave as variables, objects may have methods (functions) associated with them. These will be discussed below.

We have declared the library object as a literal:

```
var library = {
      name: "Central Library",
      fiction: 1000,
      nonfiction: 500,
      open: true };
```

Another way to create such an object uses the keyword `new`:

```
var library = new Object();
library.name = "Central Library";
library.fiction = 1000;
library.nonfiction = 500;
library.open = true;
```

Both of these declarations do the same thing. Use of the `new` keyword may be useful when the values for some properties are to be filled in at a later time. In most cases, however, the literal definition is recommended.

Note that we could also declare an empty object by a statement like the following, and add properties to the object as needed:

```
var library = {};
```

It is important to note that if an object is assigned to a variable, that variable contains a *reference* to the object, not a copy of the object itself. If a copy is made of the variable, that copy is a reference to the *same* object. If we write the following:

```
                var lib2 = library;
```

both `lib2` and `library` identify the same object. If we then write:

```
                lib2.fiction = 1200;
```

the value of `library.fiction` is also changed to 1200.

Iteration using for ... in

For some objects, it is desirable to perform an action systematically on each of its properties. This can be done by a statement similar to a for loop called the **for ... in** statement.

Given the library object discussed above, we could display each of its properties by writing:

```
for (var prop in library) {
        document.write(prop + ": " + library[prop] + "<br>");
}
```

The output of this loop should be:

```
name: Central Library
fiction: 1000
nonfiction: 500
open: true
```

In general, though, the order of the iteration cannot be guaranteed.

Methods

In object-oriented programming, functions belong to specific objects. In JavaScript, a function associated with an object is called a **method**. We have used this term in passing before, and now we are prepared to state a central principle of JavaScript:

*In JavaScript, **all** functions are methods.*

Most JavaScript methods are associated with a specific object that must be named when the method is called, such as `document.write()`. Methods that are called without naming an object are assumed to be methods of the global object.

Strictly speaking, methods are properties. Their name is the function name, and their value is the text of the function definition. If we want to add a method to the library object to count the total books, we could write:

```
library.totalBooks = function () {
    return this.fiction + this.nonfiction;
};
```

This will define a property named `totalBooks`, whether it previously existed or not, as being the stated function definition. This seems pretty straightforward, but what is meant by the keyword `this`? The answer is that `this` in any statement refers to the object to which the statement belongs. In this case, that object is `library`, and we are stating that the two values referred to in the expression are `library.fiction` and `library.nonfiction`.

Some Predefined Objects

JavaScript provides a relatively small number of predefined objects. Here we introduce two important ones: `Date` and `Math`.

The `Date` object contains a date. Internally the date is a number, representing the number of milliseconds that have elapsed since midnight on Jan. 1, 1970 Coordinated Universal Time (UTC). This number can be broken up into seven components: year, month, day, hours, minutes, seconds, and milliseconds.

Each component of the `Date` is a number. The year is the full four-digit year, and the month is a number in the range 0 (January) to 11 (December). The other values are straightforward.

The `Date` object can represent a complete date as a string, using the browser's time zone:

Sun Jan 26 2020 08:14:02 GMT-0500 (Eastern Standard Time)

Further, the `Date` object has methods that can accept such a string and parse it into its seven components.

To create a `Date` object containing the current date and time, you can write:

```
var curDate = new Date();
```

To create a `Date` object with a specific time, you can use `new Date()` with one or more arguments. For example:

```
var myDate = new Date( 2020, 0, 26, 8, 14, 2, 0);
```
creates a `Date` object with the same value as given in the string above. It is also possible to omit up to five of the trailing values, which will then default to zero.

There are methods to extract any of the parts of a Date object:

```
// Return the full (4-digit) year
var year = myDate.getFullYear();

// Return the month (0-11)
var month = myDate.getMonth();

// Return the day of the month (1-31);
var dayOfMonth = myDate.getDate();

// Return the day of the week (0-6, 0 = Sunday);
var dayOfWeek = myDate.getDay();

// Return the hour (0-23)
var hour = myDate.getHours();

// Return the minute (0-59)
var minute = myDate.getMinutes();

//Return the second (0-59)
var second = myDate.getSeconds();

// Return the millisecond (0-999)
var millisecond = myDate.getMilliseconds();
```

You can also get the raw value of the date and time, that is, the number of milliseconds since midnight Jan. 1, 1970:

```
var rawTime = myDate.getTime();
```

All the above methods return values in the local time of the browser. There are also methods to return values as UTC, to set the time values individually, to convert to and from various time formats, and to perform a number of other time-related operations.

The `Math` object provides a collection of methods to perform basic mathematical operations, along with some properties containing basic mathematical constants. `Math` is a global object that exists by default in your JavaScript environment and does not need to be created. It may be surprising to think of a collection of math functions as an object, but this is a common way to present such a collection in an object-oriented program.

The Math object provides methods to compute square roots, cube roots, and a variety of common math functions including a full range of trigonometric functions. Some of the most useful methods include:

`Math.sqrt(num)` returns the square root of the number `num`.

`Math.abs(num)` returns the absolute value of `num`.

`Math.sin(num)` returns the sine of `num`. The argument should be given in radians.

`Math.exp(num)` return the value of E (Euler's constant) to the power `num`.

`Math.log(num)` returns the natural logarithm of `num`.

`Math.min()` and `Math.max()` return the minimum and maximum, respectively, from a list of values. For example:

```
Math.min (50, 20, -10, 35) returns -10.
```

Math also provides 8 properties representing important mathematical constants:

`Math.E` gives Euler's constant.

`Math.PI` gives the value of Pi.

`Math.SQRT2` gives the square root of 2.

`Math.SQRT1_2` gives the square root of ½.

`Math.LN2` gives the natural logarithm of 2.

`Math.LN10` gives the natural logarithm of 10.

`Math.LOG2E` gives the base 2 logarithm of E.

`Math.LOG10E` gives the base 10 logarithm of E.

There are a number of other methods and properties as well.

Chapter 10: Arrays, Maps and Sets

In Chapter 3, we saw several of JavaScript's basic datatypes, including number, string, and boolean. Variables of these datatypes hold one value at a time. But there is often a need to store a set of related items in a single variable. This need can be met with some special kinds of JavaScript objects, including **arrays**, **maps** and **sets**.

What are Arrays?

An array is a variable that may contain a list of values, not just a single value. In many languages, arrays must be declared to have a fixed size and a single datatype. JavaScript arrays do not have either of these restrictions.

Suppose you want to maintain a list of your favorite classical composers. You could create such an array with the statements:

```
var composers;
composers = ['Mozart', 'Vivaldi', 'Bach', 'Tchaikovsky',
    'Dvorak'];
```

These statements create an array with five elements, each initialized to a specific name. Note that `composers` does not have to be explicitly declared to be an array. When it is initialized, it automatically becomes an array with five elements.

We have noted that JavaScript has only one non-primitive data type, the object. This statement is still `true`. An array *is* an object. However, it is an important special case, with some restrictions and a special notation. The restriction is that the names of all elements of the array, which are actually properties, must be integers. The special notation is discussed below.

Reading and Writing Array Elements

The individual elements of an array can be read or written using index numbers, beginning with zero:

```
var first = composers[0];
composers[3] = 'Debussy';
```

After this code, `first` contains the string `'Mozart'`, and the name `'Tchaikovsky'` in the array has been changed to `'Debussy'`.

What if you try to access an array element that has never been given a value? By default, all such elements have the value `undefined`.

```
var tooHigh = composers[5];
```

sets the variable `tooHigh` to `undefined`.

An array has a few properties in addition to its elements. One such property gives the length of the array. This is the number of elements the array contains, up to the highest element that has a value even if some elements are undefined. Since array indexes begin with zero, the length is the index (plus 1) of the highest element that has been given a value. If we write:

```
composerCount = composers.length;
```

then `composerCount` will have the value 5.

Managing Tables

Arrays are especially useful for storing tables of values. Consider the factorial table that was computed and output in Chapter 7. The loop structures we saw in Chapter 6 can be used with arrays to operate on all the elements of the array up to a certain limit. A few simple changes to the code could allow us to store the table in an array. Here is the new version of `fact.js`:

```
function factTable(formId) {

    // Get the limit value
    var limit = formId.textin.value;

    // Make sure limit is a valid number
    if (limit >= 1) {

        // Initialize variables
        var val = 1;
        var fact = 1;
```

```
            var index = 0;
            var factTb = [];

            // Compute values and store them in an array
            for (var count = 1; count <= limit; count++) {
                factTb[index++] = fact;
                fact = fact * ++val;
                if (fact > 999999999999999) {
                    break;
                }
            }


            // Now build the output string
            var result = "<pre>VALUE      FACTORIAL\n";
            for (var i = 0; i < factTb.length; i++) {
                val = i + 1;
                fact = factTb[i];
                result += val + "            " + fact + "\n";
            }
            result += "</pre>";

        } else {
            result = "Invalid limit!";
        }

        // output the table
        document.getElementById("textout").innerHTML = result;
    }
```

This can be run with exactly the same HTML file as before.

Note that even though the array is initially empty, it must be declared to be an array by the line:

```
        var factTb = [];
```

If you declare the name without the square brackets and then try to access one of its elements, an error will occur.

Unlike arrays in many other languages, JavaScript arrays can contain values of various datatypes at the same time. In the code above, instead of printing the table heading separately, we could have stored it as the first element of the array.

Since arrays are objects, they have a number of useful methods associated with them. We will meet a few of these next.

Adding and Removing Elements

There is often a need to add a new element after the existing elements in an array. For this purpose JavaScript provides the `push()` method, which can be used with any array:

```
composers.push('Gershwin');
```

will add the name Gershwin to the end of the `composers` array.

`push()` is a function, and like most functions, it returns a value. The value is the length of the array after the new element was added.

To remove the last element, there is a corresponding pop() method. This method deletes the last element. The value returned is the element that was deleted.

If you have worked with stacks, you will recognize that the methods push() and pop() are exactly what you need to use a JavaScript array as a pushdown stack. This is generally more difficult in other languages.

It is also possible to `push()` more than one element at a time. For example, the following statement adds two new elements:

```
composers.push('Gershwin', 'Debussy');
```

Sometimes there is also a need to add or remove elements at the beginning of the array. This requires that we shift all the existing elements up, to make room for new elements, or down, to fill in the space vacated by elements that are removed. This need can be met with the methods `shift()` (to remove an element) and `unshift()` (to add elements). Starting with the original `composers` array:

```
composers.unshift('Bernstein', 'Beethoven');
```

will change the array to:

```
['Bernstein', 'Beethoven', 'Mozart', 'Vivaldi', 'Bach',
    'Tchaikovsky', 'Dvorak'].
```

If we follow this with:

```
composers.shift();
```

then the element `'Bernstein'` will be removed. Just like the push and pop methods, the return value of unshift is the new array size, and the return value of shift is the element which has been removed.

Multidimensional Arrays

Often there is a need to use arrays to implement tables that have more than one dimension. Returning to our `composers` array, we may have a need to store additional information about each composer, such as their date of birth, nationality, favorite instrument, etc. JavaScript does not support multidimensional arrays directly, but the type of data stored in an array element can be any type, including another array. Thus, it would be possible to declare an array such as:

```
var composers = [
    ['Mozart', 1756, 'Austria'],
    ['Vivaldi', 1678, 'Italy'],
    ['Bach', 1685, 'Germany'],
    ['Tchaikovsky', 1840, 'Russia'],
    ['Dvorak', 1841, 'Czechoslovakia']
];
```

Each element in this array is referred to by the index of the subarray followed by the index within the subarray. To get the nationality for Vivaldi, for example, we would write:

```
nat = composers[1][2];
```

There is no requirement that the size of each subarray be the same, but it may be difficult to traverse all the elements in an oddly shaped array.

There are dozens of array methods that we have not yet discussed. You will learn about some of these as needed in future chapters.

Array Iteration

There is often a need to perform some action on all the elements of an array. For example, we may want to print each element, or transform each element by some arithmetic function.

One way to do this may be to use a standard **for** loop. If the array contains 50 elements, you can set the loop index to count from 1 to 50 to perform the desired operation on each element:

```
for (var index = 1; index <= 50; index++) {
    document.write(myArray[index] + "<br\>");
}
```

However, JavaScript offers two simpler ways to do this for arrays, as well as other special objects that consist of collections of values. Both ways are variations on the **for** loop. First is the **for ... of** loop, which iterates over all the elements of a collection:

```
for (var value of myArray) {
    document.write(value + "<br\>");
}
```

The second option is the **forEach** method. This statement calls a specified function once for every element in the array. `forEach` is actually a method of the array object, so the syntax is a little different:

```
myArray.forEach(myFunc);
```

```
myFunc(value) {
    document.write(value + "<br\>");
}
```

The function parameter represents the current value for the iteration. This is often a good place for a short anonymous function, which can be written directly as the argument to `forEach`.

It is also possible to use this construct to modify the content of each element, using two additional parameters:

```
myFunc(value, index, arrayName) {
    arrayName[index] = value + 1;
}
```

The additional parameters are the current index and the name of the array, respectively.

Break and Continue

You have met the `break` and `continue` statements in Chapters 5 and 6. Both statements may transfer to labeled statements in certain circumstances. Only `break` may be used with conditionals, but both statements may be used inside loops. Recall that a `break` statement exits the enclosing loop, while a `continue` statement returns to the start for the next iteration.

Labels are most useful with `break` and `continue` when there are nested loops, and this is most likely to occur when processing multidimensional arrays. Suppose for example that you need to process the elements in each row of a 2-dimensional array until a certain condition is met. This might best be done using a `for` statement to iterate over each row, with an inner `for` statement to process each element in the row. If the desired condition is met during processing, a `break` statement can be used to exit the `for` statement, but this would not exit both loops. If a label is placed on the outer `for` statement, it is possible to exit both loops by referring to this label.

Suppose you are writing a program that looks through a two-dimensional array to find the row with the smallest sum. You might write something like:

```
function findLowRow() {

    var lowSum = 999;
    var lowRow = 0;
    var rowSum = 0;
    const NUM_ROWS = 4;
    const NUM_COLS = 5;

    var table = [
    [1,2,3,4,5],
    [6,7,8,9,10],
```

```
        [0,1,0,2,3],
        [2,4,6,8,10]
     ];

     // loop through the rows
     rowLoop: for (var row=0; row < NUM_ROWS; row++) {
         rowSum = 0;
         for (var col=0; col < NUM_COLS; col++) {
             rowSum += table[row][col];
         }

         // Is this the lowest sum so far?
         if (rowSum < lowSum) {
             lowSum = rowSum;
             lowRow = row;
         }
     }

     // output the result
     var result = "Row number: " + lowRow +
         "<br>Row sum: " + lowSum + "<br>";
     document.getElementById("textout").innerHTML = result;
}
```

We are assuming that there are rows with sums less than 999.

This works but may be inefficient because it adds all the elements of every row even when the sum is clearly too large. This does not matter for this trivial array, but it may make a difference if the array is very large. To avoid this problem, we could change the loop structure as follows:

```
     // loop through the rows
     rowLoop: for (var row=0; row < NUM_ROWS; row++) {
         rowSum = 0;
         for (var col=0; col < NUM_COLS; col++) {
             rowSum += table[row][col];

             // exit this row if sum is already too large
             if (rowSum > lowSum) {
                     continue rowLoop;
             }
         }

         // Is this the lowest sum so far?
         if (rowSum < lowSum) {
             lowSum = rowSum;
             lowRow = row;
         }
```

```
}
```

The `continue` statement causes the program to go on to the next row as soon as the sum gets too large. The label is necessary here; without it the program would continue with the inner loop, which means it would stay on the same row.

Save this program in a file named `label.js` and test it using the following simple HTML file:

```
<!DOCTYPE html>
<html>
<head>
    <title>JavaScript Demo Page</title>
</head>
<body>
    <script src=label.js></script>

    <h1>JavaScript Demo Page<h1>
    <h2>Label Demo</h1>

    <button onClick="findlowrow()">Run</button>

    <br><br>
    The result:<br>
    <p id="textout"></p>
     <br>

</body>
</html>
```

In a similar way, the `break` statement may be used with a label when the logic requires it.

Note that `break` and `continue`, with or without labels, may be used from within a `for ... of` statement as well. They may *not* be used within a `forEach` statement since the order of iteration is unpredictable.

Maps and Sets

Arrays are not the only kind of JavaScript object specialized to contain collections of values. Two additional types of collections were added in ES-2015: maps and sets.

Maps may be viewed essentially as collections of name-value (or key-value) pairs similar to object literals. Unlike arrays, maps may have keys of any datatype, even other objects. In addition, the `forEach` method may be used to iterate over their elements. Maps guarantee that iteration will take place in the order in which items were originally stored.

Sets are essentially arrays that are guaranteed to contain only unique values. They can also be iterated using `forEach`, but the order is unspecified.

Chapter 11: Events, Timers, and Errors

Early web pages, driven by HTML alone, were static. They may have been beautiful or full of information, but they did not change. The only way to go beyond a web page was to click a link that caused the server to switch to a new page altogether.

Today as we know it, web pages are expected to respond in many ways when something happens. That something is called an **event**.

The most familiar events involve user actions affecting form elements on the page, such as typing in a text box or clicking a button. The browser itself can also be a source of events, such as when it finishes loading a page.

Objects that can trigger events, such as buttons, are created by HTML. Many responses might be needed to these events, including changes to the HTML and even to the CSS. However, HTML cannot provide these responses, this is the job of JavaScript.

HTML Events

Events can be handled in a web page only if they are first triggered or detected by the HTML code. Various HTML elements have attributes intended to specify a response to an event. These attributes generally start with the syllable `on`, followed by the name of the event. For example, `onload` is an attribute of the `<body>` tag that specifies an action when the page has finished loading.

There are many attributes of this type. A few examples include:

Attribute	Tag	Event
onload	`<body>`	page has finished loading
onafterprint	`<body>`	page has been printed
onpagehide	`<body>`	user has left the page
oninput	text fields	input has been typed
onfocus	various	the object has been selected
onkeydown	various	a key has been pressed
onmouseover	various	the mouse or pointer moves over the object

The value of these attributes specifies what to do when the event occurs. This is usually a JavaScript function or a very short sequence of JavaScript code.

Handling Events

When an event occurs, control is passed to the JavaScript function or code defined to handle that event. We have seen examples of this in Chapter 7, on our demo web page:

```
<button id="run_button"
        onclick="factTable(inform)">Run</button>
```

The function `factTable` is assumed to be found inside the `<script>` tags.

Suppose we want to add a display of the current date and time to our Demo page introduced in Chapter 7. Consider the example that creates a factorial table. We first need to add a place in the HTML file for the date to be shown:

```
<!DOCTYPE html>
<html>
<head>
    <title>JavaScript Demo Page</title>
    <link rel="stylesheet" type="text/css"
            href="fact.css">
</head>
<body>
    <script src="fact.js"></script>

    <h1>JavaScript Demo Page</h1>
    <h2>Factorial table</h2>
    <p id="today">PLACE DATE HERE</p>

    <form id="inform">
        Enter an upper bound for the factorial table:<br/>
        <input type="text" id="textin">

    </form>

    <br/>
    <button id="run_button"
        onClick="factTable(inform)">Run</button>

    <br/><br/>
    The factorial table:<br/>
    <p id="textout"></p>

    <br/>

</body>
```

To set the date in this element, we need a line of code in the JavaScript file. Place this line ahead of the function definitions:

```
document.getElementById("today").innerHTML = new Date();
```

Now when we load the HTML page, we should find that the date appears:

JavaScript Demo Page

Factorial table

Tue Mar 03 2020 15:42:57 GMT-0500 (Eastern Standard Time)

Enter an upper bound for the factorial table:

[Run]

The factorial table:

The date appears in the default format provided by the Date object. With a little more work, we could change the format to whatever we prefer.

If the date does not appear, check that your `<script>` element is at the end of the HTML `<body>`, not at the beginning. Otherwise, the page might be rendered before there is a chance to insert the date.

Event Listeners

There is one aspect of the event handling methods above that is not too satisfying. We've tried to keep all of the JavaScript completely separate from the HTML, but here we are defining HTML tag attributes that include JavaScript code.

To avoid even this slight aberration, we can define **event listeners** in the JavaScript code. Using listeners, we eliminate the `on ...` attributes in the HTML tags that contain

JavaScript. Instead, we ask JavaScript to slip them in silently and invisibly when the page loads.

In the factorial example, we can eliminate the `onclick` attribute for the Run button, and instead place the following line in the JavaScript file:

```
document.getElementById("run_button").addEventListener
        ("click", () => factTable(inform));
```

The first argument for `addEventListener` is the event name *without* the prefix "on". The second argument is the JavaScript function recast as an arrow function; the reasons for this are beyond the scope of our discussion.

Timers

JavaScript provides two functions to generate a time delay. These functions are methods of the global window object. They will call a specified function when the time is up.

`setTimeout(function, interval)` takes as parameters a function name and a time interval in milliseconds. When the specified time is up, the function will be called. `setInterval(function, interval)` works exactly the same way, but the function repeats after each interval.

Each of these methods returns a value, which can be used to stop the timer if necessary. Stopping requires two additional functions, `clearTimeout(retval)` and `clearInterval(retval)`. These can be called with the value returned by `setTimeout()` or `setInterval()` to stop those two timers, respectively.

Errors

When JavaScript code encounters a problem it cannot handle, it signals an error. Up to now, the effect of errors has been simply that the program does not work. You almost surely have encountered this behavior more than once while trying out these examples.

However, JavaScript actually has a robust error handling mechanism similar to that found in other modern languages, where these errors are generally called **exceptions**. This includes a **try ... catch ... finally** statement plus the ability to throw exceptions.

Consider the JavaScript function from Chapter 7 to compute the square of a number:

```
function findSquare(formId) {

    // Get the input value
    var inputNum = formId.textin.value;

    // If valid, compute its square
    var result;
    if (inputNum >= 1 && inputNum <= 10) {
        result = inputNum*inputNum;

    // Otherwise, store an error message
    } else {
        result = "Invalid number!";
    }

    // Display the result
    document.getElementById("textout").innerHTML = result;

}
```

What if, when typing this program, you mistyped `formId` as `formid`? Try making this change, then re-run the program. The demo page appears, but when you click the run button nothing happens. The JavaScript interpreter has come across the unknown identifier and has given up!

It would be better if we at least knew what happened. Using `try ... catch`, we can tell JavaScript to display a message before it gives up. This message could help us diagnose the problem.

```
function findSquare(formId) {

        // try this, but watch for errors
        try {

            // Get the input value (with misspelling)
            var inputNum = formid.textin.value;

            // If valid, compute its square
            var result;
            if (inputNum >= 1 && inputNum <= 10) {
                result = inputNum*inputNum;

            // Otherwise, store an error message
            } else {
```

```
              result = "Invalid number!";
        }

        // If an error was detected, display a message
    } catch(err) {
        result = err.message;
    }

    // Display the result (we're still alive!)
    document.getElementById("textout").innerHTML =
        result;

    }
```

Store this version in `square.js` and rerun `square.html`. Then enter a value and click Run. What happens now?

Your page should look like this:

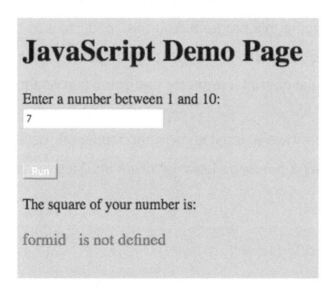

Instead of an answer, an "Invalid number" message, or nothing, you get a message that tells you exactly what is wrong with the program. This should be very helpful to you, the programmer. You should fix this promptly because this message would not be very helpful to the end user!

But where did this message come from? It turns out that when JavaScript detects an error, it creates an **error object** with all the information it can provide to help you understand the problem. You just have to request this object. You do this by setting it as a parameter in the `catch` clause.

The error object has two properties: `message` and `name`. The `message` property provides details about the error. The `name` property classifies the error into a few distinct categories. The name for the error we have just seen is `ReferenceError`.

It is also possible to follow the catch clause with another clause named `finally`. For instance, we could write:

```
// If an error was detected, display a message
} catch(err) {
    result = err.message;

// Do this no matter what
} finally {

    // Display the result (we're still alive!)
    document.getElementById("textout").innerHTML =
        result;
}
```

This would ensure that the result is displayed whether an error was detected or not. In this function that is already the case, so the `finally` clause is unnecessary.

It is also possible to make your own exception. The JavaScript statement:

```
throw value;
```

causes an unconditional exception. The value, which can be any type, is passed to the catch clause by default.

No error object is created automatically, but you can make your own. Also, if you catch an exception, but choose not to handle it, you can "rethrow it" to be handled at a higher level.

Chapter 12: More about Data and Expressions

This chapter discusses some JavaScript features we have not seen before, including more about numbers, data types, operators, and expressions.

Number Literals

We have seen several ways to write number literals, including:

27	integer
27.12	decimal form
2.7e5	exponential form

We know that internally, JavaScript represents all numbers as floating points. Specifically, the standard "IEEE format" is used with 64 bits. This may seem like a bad idea, since:

- 64 bits is a lot of space for small numbers, and
- Integers should be exact, while floating point may involve approximations.

These problems are avoided, though, in two ways:

- JavaScript implementations may actually use more compact forms internally when possible, and
- JavaScript guarantees that integers *are* exact, at least up to a magnitude of 2**53 (which is pretty big).

Sometimes we will want to treat a number as an integer, no matter how it is stored internally. It turns out that we can sometimes treat numbers as **2's complement** signed integers, even though they still have the single "number" datatype. The only thing that must be true about an integer is that it is a whole number (positive or negative) with no fraction part.

To understand 2's complement, think of an integer as a sequence of bits, representing a value in base 2, with the leftmost bit giving the sign (0 means positive, 1 means negative. To reverse the sign of a 2's complement number, we complement (reverse) each bit, then add 1.

It is especially necessary to think in integers if we want to express a number with a different base. All of our numbers so far have been written in base 10 (decimal). But JavaScript also allows number literals to be written in base 2, 8, or 16:

Base	Example
2 (binary)	0b11101011
8 (octal)	0o27451362
16 (hexadecimal)	0x39FA2CD6

Numbers written in this way are usually meant to be thought of as sequences of bits or **bit strings**. For historical reasons, we occasionally use octal format, where each digit represents three bits, or hexadecimal format, where each digit represents four bits. We usually want to treat these values as bit strings, usually consisting of 32 bits.

Bitwise Operators

Why think of a number as a bit string? One reason is so we can view each bit as a boolean value, representing either `true` or `false`. To support this, JavaScript gives us a set of bitwise operators that we have not seen before. These operators act on each bit of two input values to produce a single bit in the result:

Operator	Purpose	Example
&	bitwise and	`1010 & 0011 equals 0010`
|	bitwise or	`1010	0011 equals 1011`
^	bitwise exclusive or	`1010 ^ 0011 equals 1001`

The **bitwise and** sets each output bit to 1 only if *both* input bits are 1, otherwise 0. The **bitwise or** sets each output bit to 1 if *either* input bit is 1. The **bitwise exclusive or** sets each output bit to 1 only if the input bits are *different.* It is important not to confuse the bitwise operators `&` and `|` with the similar boolean operators `&&` and `||` which compare boolean values.

In addition to these operators, we have a unary **not** operator that complements each bit:

Operator	Purpose	Example
~	bitwise not	`~1010 equals 0101`

and three different binary **shift operators** that move an entire bit string to a given number of positions left or right:

Operator	Purpose	Example
`>>`	signed right shift	`10100011 >> 2 equals 11101000`
`>>>`	unsigned right shift	`10100011 >>> 2 equals 00101000`
`<<`	left shift	`10100011 << 2 equals 10001100`

The signed right shift moves all the bits to the right, discarding the bits on the right, and copying the leftmost bit into the empty spaces on the left. If the value is viewed as a signed 2's complement integer, then each shift is equivalent to dividing by 2.

The unsigned right shift moves all the bits to the right, discarding the bits on the right, and filling the empty space with zeros. This may be useful for scanning a bit string one bit or a few bits at a time.

The single left shift moves all the bits to the left, discarding the bits at the left end and filling the empty space with zeros. This may be used to multiply by 2 or for scanning bits. It will work the same in either case.

All bitwise operators take bit strings of 32 bits as input and produce a 32-bit string as a result. If the original operands are numbers, they are automatically converted to 32-bit strings before performing the operation. This is just one example of implicit type conversion that will be discussed next.

Type Conversion

On many occasions, a function or an operator expects arguments of a certain type, while the values available are of a different type. We would like to change the type of the argument. Sometimes, perhaps due to an error, this is not possible; if the original argument is the string `"abc"` there is no way to convert this to a `number`. But very often a meaningful conversion can be made.

In some cases, as in our example in Chapter 4, we need to call a function to explicitly change a type:

```
oldWeight = "50";
netWeight = Number(oldWeight) + 20;
```

Here we had to convert the string `oldWeight` to a `number` type, or the expression would have performed string concatenation instead of addition.

JavaScript also gives us the functions `String()` to convert a value to a `string` type, and `Boolean()` to convert a value to a `boolean` type. Note the uppercase first letter for the functions, and the lowercase first letter for the primitive types they return.

In many cases, JavaScript will determine what types are required as arguments for an operator or a function, and implicitly change to the needed type. We already know that the expression `"100" - 25` will produce the number 75, because the string `"100"` will be converted to a number. In most cases conversions between the three main primitive types are automatic, but there are a few surprises:

- Any non-empty string, even "0", when converted to boolean becomes true.
- The empty string "", converted to a number, becomes 0.
- The value null, converted to a number, becomes 0.

Because of these and other unexpected conversions, it may be better to use explicit type conversion as much as possible.

The typeof Operator

`typeof` is a unary operator (not a function) that takes a value of any type as an argument and returns a string identifying the type of that value. For example:

`typeof "Hello"` -- returns `"string"`

`typeof 2.718` -- returns `"number"`

`typeof true` -- returns `"boolean"`

When applied to the main primitive types, the behavior of `typeof` is straightforward. We also have:

`typeof function() {}` -- returns `"function"`

Almost anything else returns `"object"`:

```
typeof  [1, 2, 3] returns "object"
typeof { breed: "terrier", color: "brown"} returns "object"
```
and surprisingly,
```
typeof null returns "object"
```

The `typeof` operator returns `"object"` for most "special" objects, including arrays, maps, and the `Date` object. `typeof` cannot be used to distinguish these objects.

Methods for Searching Strings

For many reasons, you might want to search a text string to find all occurrences of a certain substring, say, `"green"`. In some cases, if you have decided you don't like green, you might want to replace every instance of `"green"` with `"red"`.

JavaScript provides several methods for this purpose. These are methods of the `string` type (if this sounds strange, see the next chapter). Suppose we want to find the substring `"green"` in the following string:

```
"When the light is green, go!"
```

We could write the following statements:

```
var lightStr = "When the light is green, go!";
pos = lightStr.search("green");
```

This method returns the *position* of the first character in the substring (starting from zero). After these statements, `pos` would have the value 18.

If the string is not found, the method returns -1.

We don't actually need the variable `lightStr`. We could also write:
```
pos = ("When the light is green, go!").search("green");
```
but this is more awkward and is seldom used.

What if `"green"` occurs more than once? For example, what would be the result of the following statements:

94

```
var homeStr = "The green, green grass of home";
pos = homeStr.search("green");
```

The result in this case would be 4. If there is more than one instance of the substring, `search()` finds only the first.

Now that we found our substring, we sometimes want to change it. The `replace()` method is designed for this. if we write:

```
var lightStr = "When the light is green, go!";
var newStr = lightStr.replace("green", "red");
```

The value of `newStr` would now be `"When the light is red, go!"`, which is probably not a good idea!

In this example we had only one instance of the target substring. If the existing substring given as the first argument is an ordinary string, and occurs more than once, only the first instance will be replaced.

There is another string method that does pretty much the same thing as `search()`. If we write:

```
var valleyStr = "How green was my valley";
pos = valleyStr.indexOf("green");
```

We will get 4 for the answer. And if we write:

```
var homeStr = "The green, green grass of home";
pos = homeStr.lastIndexOf("green");
```

The program will set pos to 11, the starting position of the last occurrence of the string `"green"`.

All of these searches are case sensitive. If `valleyStr` is changed to `"How Green was my Valley"`, a match will not be found.

Are some of these methods redundant, since they seem to do the same thing? It turns out that `search()` can do a lot more, but it may take a little longer to do it. `replace()` can do more as well. More about this in the next section.

Regular Expressions

Expressions in JavaScript normally represent a single value that can be stored in a variable or used as a function argument. A regular expression is something different: a type of expression that can represent many different values at once.

Regular expressions came about because of the need to find certain patterns in strings. For example, we may be searching through a large amount of text containing email addresses. We want to flag all addresses from Canada. These addresses normally end in "`.ca`".

We could represent these addresses using the familiar wild card notation as "`*.ca`". Here "`*`" is commonly used to represent any possible string, so "`*.ca`" is a pattern that matches any string at all ending in "`.ca`". This is too general because it has no information about where these email addresses begin. To find the beginning, we should note that an email address is usually preceded by a space (or the beginning of a line) and always contains the character "`@`". So, our complete pattern could be

```
" *@*.ca"
```

This is better, but it does not cover the case where the address is at the beginning of a line, nor does it reflect that the strings before and after the "@" must not be empty. We need more than just the wild card character; we really need a complete notation for patterns. This notation is called a **regular expression**.

A regular expression in JavaScript is a pattern string enclosed in slashes ("/"), possibly followed by one or more flag characters. The slashes tell the interpreter that this *is* a regular expression because methods like `search()` and `replace()` take arguments that may be either strings or regular expressions.

In the simplest case, we might have the regular expression `/green/`, but this just represents the string "`green`" (and note that there are no quotes).

Adding flags is one way we can invoke the added power of regular expressions:

- The flag "`i`" indicates a pattern that is *insensitive* to case. If we write:

```
var valleyStr = "How Green was my Valley";
```

```
pos = valleyStr.search(/green/i);
```

The pattern will match the string "Green" because the uppercase letter does not matter.

- The flag "g" indicates *global* matching or replacement. *All* instances of the pattern will be matched. If we write:

```
var homeStr = "The green, green grass of home";
var newStr = homeStr.replace(/green/g, "red");
```

The result will be "The red, red grass of home".

The string between the slashes can also include a number of special codes. For example:

- [abc] matches any single character that is an "a", a "b", or a "c"
- [^abc] matches any single character that is *not* one of the above
- [a-j] matches any of the first ten characters of the alphabet

There are also a variety of special codes called **metacharacters** that have special meaning, such as:

- ^ represents the beginning of the string
- $ represents the end of the string
- \s represents any whitespace, such as spaces and tabs
- \d matches any digit (this is the same as [0-9])
- \w matches any letter, digit, or underscore (same as [a-zA-Z0-9_])
- \b matches the beginning or end of a word (i.e. a **word boundary**)

And there are some codes called **quantifiers** that indicate how many times a preceding regular expression should occur, such as:

- * means zero or more times (note that this is a different meaning for the traditional wildcard character)
- + means one or more times (but not zero)
- ? means either zero times or one time
- {N} means exactly N times

For each of these, the preceding regular expression is either a single character or a complete expression enclosed in parentheses.

With tools like these, we should be able to represent our desired email addresses as a regular expression:

```
/\b\w+@\w+.ca\b/
```

This indicates that an address of the desired format starts at a word boundary, and includes one or more letters, digits, or underscores, followed by an "at" ("@") character, followed again by one or more letters, digits, or underscores, followed by the sequence ".ca", and ending at another word boundary. This is somewhat simplified; for example, it ignores the fact that there could be extra periods in the address.

For another example, let's create a pattern representing a U.S. telephone number. Such numbers may optionally begin with the U.S. country code "+1", followed by a space. The remainder of the number has the form `(ddd) ddd-dddd`, where each "d" represents a digit. This can be represented as:

```
/\b(+1 )?\(\d{3}\) \d{3}-\d{4}\b/
```

This expression indicates that the pattern to be matched begins with an optional string "+1 " (with one space only) followed by a sequence of digits and other characters in the form shown. The parentheses "(" and ")" need to be preceded by backslashes to avoid their usual special meaning inside the expression.

As a companion to `search()`, JavaScript also provides the method `match()`. This method returns an array containing all the strings actually matched. If we have the string:

```
var phoneStr = "My phone number is (304) 555-1212
        and my brother's phone number is +1 (222) 999-3456"
```

Then the value of the expression:

```
phoneStr.match(/\b(+1 )?\(\d{3}\) \d{3}-\d{4}\b/g)
```

will be `["(304) 555-1212", "+1 (222) 999-3456"]`

This is not a complete reference for regular expressions or string matching. There are many other aspects that are beyond the scope of this discussion. One thing we have yet to mention, is that like most entities in Java, regular expressions are actually objects! More about this in the next chapter.

Chapter 13: Working with Objects

You now know that most data items in JavaScript are objects. You have worked with the JavaScript object model, which is similar, but not identical to that of other languages. JavaScript does not have all of the elements that might be expected for true object-oriented programming, but there is a lot to the JavaScript model that we have not yet seen. Let's review what we know so far.

Objects consist of properties, in the form of name-value pairs, also called key-value pairs. We may declare objects as literals, listing their properties explicitly, as in our library example from Chapter 9:

```
var library = {
    name: "Central Library",
    fiction: 1000,
    nonfiction: 500,
    open: true };
```

Here we have created a single object with four properties and declared initial values for them.

These properties are all primitive JavaScript types, but properties may be of any type, including other objects. In particular, functions are types of objects, so a function definition may be the value of an object property. Properties that are functions are called methods of the object. For example, one way that we expanded the library object was by adding the method `totalBooks`:

```
library.totalBooks = function () {
    return this.fiction + this.nonfiction;
};
```

`totalBooks()` is now both a property and a method of `library`. If we want to get the value of `totalBooks` we can write:

```
count = library.totalBooks();
```

In classical object-oriented programming, objects can be accessed only through their methods. In JavaScript, however, we generally have direct access to object properties as well.

Objects can be declared using an object literal, which makes sense when we need a single object and at least some of its properties are known when the program is written. But properties may also be given values at a later time, and new ones may be added.

We have also seen another way to create an object, using the keyword **new**:

```
var library = new Object();
```

This statement dynamically creates an object which is initially empty. We can then add properties and give them values through statements like the following:

```
library.name = "Central Library";
library.fiction = 1000;
```

Now it is time to learn more about JavaScript objects.

Constructors and Prototypes

One thing you might have missed in the statement:

```
var library = new Object();
```

is the term `Object()`, which seems to actually be a function. What is this?

The answer is that `Object()` is a special kind of function called a **constructor**. When an object is created using `new`, a function is called that creates that object. The `Object()` function creates a new, empty object.

It is also possible to create your own constructor. Moreover, you could include a set of initial property values as parameters to the constructor function. If you need several objects to represent different libraries, you could write:

```
function Library( nm, fic, nonfic, op) {
    this.name = nm;
    this.fiction = fic;
    this.nonfiction = nonfic;
    this.open = op;
}
```

Notice the use of the keyword **this**. Remember that `this` generally refers to the function or object that the statement is contained in. If we call this function with the following code:

```
lib2 = new Library("North Library", 2500, 1500, false);
```

we have created a new object `lib2` with the specified properties.

Constructor functions can be useful, but they do not support the classical model of object construction and inheritance. In that model, an object is an instance of a **class**, which defines the object's properties (or methods). Further, the class is a **subclass** of a parent, called the **superclass**. The class (and all of its objects) is said to *inherit* the properties of the superclass. Every superclass has its own superclass, forming a **chain** until the top-level class is reached, which is generally called the **object** class.

Also, if changes are made to a class or any of the super classes in its chain, these changes are reflected in the objects created from that class.

On the surface, JavaScript does not conform to this model very well. There is no obvious relation between objects we create and other objects, except the object implicitly defined by a constructor. There is no way, it seems, to inherit properties from another object. Or is there?

It turns out that JavaScript objects have a built-in property called a **prototype**. The prototype of an object points to another object (possibly `null`) from which it inherits properties. The prototype, in turn, may have its own prototype, forming a chain just as above, until a null prototype is reached.

Before ES-2015, the prototype existed, but was hidden with no decent way to access it directly. Today, it is possible to create an object with another object explicitly designated as its prototype. In addition, an existing prototype can be retrieved and modified.

Suppose in the library example we have a collection of methods that are common to all libraries. Without prototypes, we would have to define these methods separately in every constructor or in every object literal. Not only does this clutter our program, but it might take up unnecessary storage with multiple copies of the same methods. Further, any change needed in these methods would have to be made separately in each constructor or object.

Using prototypes, we can create and declare a single instance of methods or other properties that are common to multiple objects or object types. In our simple example, we could declare:

```
var libMethods = {
        totalBooks: function () {
                return this.fiction + this.nonfiction;
        }
}
```

This object could serve as a prototype for both `library` and `lib2`, avoiding duplication. The method `totalBooks()` will be inherited from the prototype. This may seem trivial in this case but could be very important if a large set of functions is shared by many objects.

Some languages support the concept of multiple inheritance, by which an object, through its class, can inherit properties from more than one superclass. This concept is not supported in JavaScript.

How do we make `libMethods` a prototype of these other objects? It is necessary to use a new object method to create objects with an explicit prototype. This method is called `Object.create()`. The first parameter for this function is the prototype object (possibly null). If we have defined `libMethods`, then we can write:

```
lib2 = Object.create(libMethods);
```

This statement creates an object `lib2` that initially contains the `totalBooks()` property. Any further properties would need to be added explicitly.

Alternately, if we want to add additional properties on creation, we can add a second parameter to `Object.create()` which has the form of an object literal:

```
lib2 = Object.create(

    libMethods,

    {

        name: "North Library"

    }

)
```

This creates an object that initially contains both the `totalBooks()` method and the `name` property. Other properties can be added later.

There are several things you should know about object construction with prototypes. In this example:

- `totalBooks()` is treated as a property of `lib2`, just like its own properties.

- If `lib2` has its own property with the name `totalBooks`, that property will override the `totalBooks()` property in the prototype.

- If we add a new method to the prototype `libMethods`, this method becomes available to all objects that have `libMethods` in their prototype chain.

- If we try to change a property that is defined in a prototype, we actually create a property with the same name in our specific object. The prototype is not changed.

- Suppose, for example, we add a new property `reference` to `lib2`, and then change the method `totalBooks()` to include this category. We could write:

```
lib2.totalBooks = function() {
    return this.fiction + this.nonfiction +
        this.reference; }
```

`lib2` now contains its own `totalBooks()` method that overrides the method in the prototype.

Note also that the only properties that should be defined in a prototype are methods and constants. It would not make sense to define a value that is intended to be changed, since any change would convert that property to a property of the individual object.

More about "new"

You know that one way to create an object is to use the keyword **new**. For example:

```
var library = new Object();
```

This is a very common way if not the only way to dynamically create new objects or data structures in many languages. Now it is time to mention that the use of new in JavaScript is usually a bad idea.

The biggest problem is that object creation using new in JavaScript can be costly in time and space, and there are almost always other ways to do it. JavaScript has evolved greatly over the years, and it sometimes gives you too many ways to do things!

For example, two other ways to create a library object are:

```
var library = {}   or
var library = Object.create(null);
```

The first method declares an object that is initially empty, but we can add properties later. The second method dynamically creates an object and optionally specifies a prototype. Both methods are usually preferable to the use of new.

Another problem with new is that it can be accidentally left out, leading to unexpected results but often no actual error. For example, if we write:

```
lib2 = Library("North Library", 2500, 1500, false);
```

instead of

```
lib2 = new Library("North Library", 2500, 1500, false);
```

we will wind up executing the constructor function immediately instead of creating a new object. This constructor, like many, changes values using the keyword this. The changes here could end up being made to the wrong values and could cause obscure errors.

For these reasons, we will prefer using:

```
var composers = ['Mozart', 'Vivaldi', 'Bach',        'Tchaikovsky',
    'Dvorak'];
```

instead of:

```
var composers = new Array ('Mozart', 'Vivaldi', 'Bach',
        'Tchaikovsky', 'Dvorak');
```

to create arrays, although these statements do exactly the same thing.

Another use of `new` that is usually discouraged is to use it as a wrapper to make objects out of primitive types. The following statements are legal JavaScript:

```
numObj = new Number(500);
strObj = new String("Hello!");
boolObj = new Boolean(true);
```

Each of these statements calls a constructor to create an object whose value is a primitive type. Why would you want to do this? The usual reason is that primitive types cannot have properties, while these objects can. But didn't we introduce methods like `str.search()` in the last chapter, where `str` is a primitive string? Yes, we did, and it worked! The secret is that when we reference methods or properties of a primitive type data item, JavaScript silently promotes the data item to an object, and applies the property reference. We can write:

```
grassLen = ("The green, green grass of home").length;
```
or
```
valStr = (357).toString();
```

and these statements will work as expected.

We should note finally that there are some situations in which the use of the `new` keyword is preferred or necessary. For example, the statement:

```
var d = new Date();
```
is the only way to create a `Date` object.

JavaScript Classes

Since objects can be created with prototypes, we have much of the functionality of classes. Still, ES-2015 introduced the JavaScript **class** as a specific new construct.

A class in JavaScript is a type of function. In fact, the class requires one function, a constructor, which must have the name `constructor`:

```
class Library {
    constructor(libName) {
    this.name = libName;
  }
}
```

The class is "called" like a function; this actually has the effect of calling the constructor. A constructor is a special function that is used to create and initialize an object. The constructor in this example sets a property of the class called `name` to the value of the argument passed to the constructor.

Methods in classes may be declared static. Such methods are applied to the class itself, not to the objects created from it.

The class concept is an attempt to mimic the behavior of classes in a fully object-oriented language. It actually adds no new functionality but may provide a more convenient syntax.

Accessors

Most object-oriented languages offer special methods called **getters** and **setters** to provide access to object properties. Getters return the value of a property, while setters initialize or modify that value. These are often the only way to access the values of object properties. In JavaScript, object properties may in general be accessed directly. Still, getters and setters may be included in an object definition. These functions collectively are called accessors.

For example, our familiar library object could be defined as:

```
var library = {
    name: "Central Library",
    fiction: 1000,
    nonfiction: 500,
    open: true,
    totalBooks: function () {
```

```
        return this.fiction + this.nonfiction;
    }
};
```

or we could write:

```
var library = {
    name: "Central Library",
    fiction: 1000,
    nonfiction: 500,
    open: true,
    get totalBooks() {
        return this.fiction + this.nonfiction;
    }
}
```

The difference is that we now have a getter function for `totalBooks`. Although everything looks almost the same, we would now refer to the property as `library.totalBooks`, treating it as a property, not a method.

Is Everything an Object?

In JavaScript, pretty much. To drive the point home, we noted at the end of the previous chapter that even regular expressions are actually objects. To make this apparent, we could write things like:

```
var emailAddr = new RegExp(/\b\w+@\w+.ca\b/);
```

But in fact, the statement below does the same thing:

```
var emailAddr = /\b\w+@\w+.ca\b/;
```

Since `emailAddr` is an object, we can make use of its methods, including the special methods `test()` and `exec()`. The following expression will return true or false depending on whether the string in parentheses matches the pattern (in this case it does not):

```
emailAddr.test("abcde.com")
```

The following expression will return an array containing each of the actual substrings matched:

```
var homeStr = "The green, green grass of home";
var pattern = /green/g;
pattern.exec(homeStr);
```

Chapter 14: The DOM and the BOM

The **Document Object Model** (**DOM**) was introduced in Chapter 7, and we have been making limited use of this model for input and output. In this chapter, we explore this model more extensively, along with the **Browser Object Model** (**BOM**) that represents more specifically the content appearing in the browser window. These two models are part of HTML, not JavaScript, but they provide JavaScript with the basis for navigation among the document and browser elements in order to perform its requested actions.

The Document Object Model

A web page, as we know, is defined by an HTML document. The complete content of a document is an HTML element surrounded by the tags `<html>...</html>`. Most elements have their own start tag and end tag, and all HTML elements are nested inside other elements, forming a tree. This tree is called the DOM tree. The figure below illustrates this structure for a simple web page.

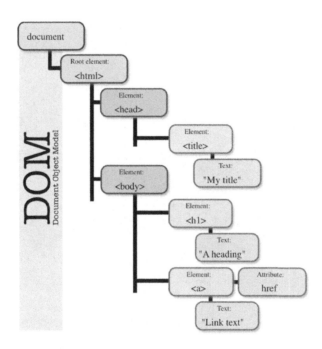

All HTML elements in a document are **nodes** of the DOM tree. There are also nodes that represent attributes, and nodes that represent comments.

The purpose of the DOM is to enable programs running in the browser (typically in JavaScript, possibly in other languages) with the ability to identify and manipulate specific elements or groups of elements within a document. Some of the things that a program may want to do with specific elements include:

- Find an element or a group of elements
- Read and write the content of an element
- Read and write element attributes
- Modify element styles
- Add and remove elements
- Handle an event at an element

The DOM is defined by standards originally managed by the World Wide Web Consortium (W3C), but currently maintained by the **Web Hypertext Application Technology Working Group (WHATWG)**. The DOM standard presents an object-oriented model of the DOM tree structure and defines a large collection of methods and interfaces for manipulating documents and their elements. These methods and interfaces support all of the actions listed above, and more.

WHATWG manages the DOM standard as a **living standard** and updates it very frequently. As a result, not all components of the standard are supported by all browsers. However, much of the DOM standard is well established and provides the core mechanism for JavaScript or other languages to dynamically interact with web documents.

The WHATWG DOM is defined in a very general way that can support languages other than JavaScript, and even web document languages other than HTML. A complete reference for the latest W3C version of the JavaScript HTML DOM can be found at https://www.w3schools.com/js/js_htmldom.asp.

JavaScript and the DOM

JavaScript programs work with the DOM using two main objects:

1. The `document` object, representing the entire document
2. The `element` object, representing individual elements

The Document Object

We have already met the `document` object in earlier chapters. Its principal use is to provide a reference to locate specific elements on a page.

The `document` object has about two dozen methods and a similar number of properties. We used one such method early in the book, `document.write()`. This method displays some text but replaces the entire document to do it.

The next step, introduced in Chapter 7, was to use a different method `document.getElementByID()`, to both read and write text within a single document element. Let's look more closely at this and other `document` methods.

Consider one of our simplest examples from Chapter 7, finding the square of a number. Here is the final HTML file for that example:

```
<!DOCTYPE html>
<html>
<head>
    <title>Find Squares</title>
    <link rel="stylesheet" type="text/css"
        href="square.css">
</head>
<body>
    <script src="square.js"></script>

    <h1>JavaScript Demo: Squaring a Number</h1>

    <!-- Ask user for an input number -->
    <form id="inform">
        Enter a number between 1 and 10:<br>
        <input type="text" id="textin">
    </form>
    <br>

    <!-- Process the input with JavaScript -->
    <button onClick="findSquare(inform)">Run</button>
    <br><br>

    <!-- Display the output (supplied by JavaScript) -->
    The square of your number is:<br>
    <p id="textout"></p>
    <br>

</body>
</html>
```

We assume that an appropriate `square.css` style file, such as that described in Chapter 7, is provided. The JavaScript file `square.js` is:

```javascript
function findSquare() {

    // Get the input value
    var innum = document.getElementById("textin").value;

    // If valid, compute its square
    var result;
    if (innum >= 1 && innum <= 10) {
        result = innum*innum;

    // Otherwise, store an error message
    } else {
        result = "Invalid number!";
    }

    // Display the result
    document.getElementById("textout").innerHTML = result;
}
```

The `document.getElementByID()` method returns an `element` object representing the HTML element with the specified `id` attribute, assuming that this element exists and is unique. Here it is used to identify the element with `id="textin"` to read the input, and to identify the element with `id="textout"` to write the output.

Note that the element itself is not the same as its content. The `"textin"` element is an `<input>` element. This element has no content, but the input value is obtained by accessing its `value` attribute. The `"textout"` element is of type `<p>` (paragraph). The content of this type of element can be read or written via the attribute `innerHTML`.

There are several other `document` methods that can be used to locate HTML elements. These include:

- `getElementsByName(name)`: Get all elements that have the given `name` attribute
- `getElementsByClassName(class)`: Get all elements that have the given `class` attribute
- `getElementsByTagName(tag)`: Get all elements that have the given tag type. The tag should be specified as a string, all uppercase.

Notice the term `Elements` in the above names. Unlike `getElementByID()`, these methods are designed to get *multiple* elements. Instead of returning an element object, they return an `HTMLCollection`. This is a special type of object, similar to an array, that has only one property and two methods. The property, `length`, can be used to determine how many elements are in the collection. The methods are:

- `item(index)`: returns the element at the specified `index` position, if any. Otherwise returns `null`. Elements are indexed starting at 0, in the order that they appear on the page.

- `namedItem(id)`: returns the item whose `id` attribute matches the given `id`. If there is no match, the `name` attribute is also checked. Otherwise returns `null`.

Strictly speaking, the index order for the items is based on a depth-first traversal of the tree. This usually corresponds to textual order.

For example, suppose that the body of an HTML document contains:

```
<body>
<h1 class="heading">This is the first heading</h1>
<p>This is paragraph one</p>
<p>This is paragraph two</p>
<h2 class="heading">This is the second heading</h2>
<p>This is paragraph three</p>
<p>This is paragraph four</p>
</body>
```

Then the JavaScript sequence:

```
var coll1 = document.getElementsByClassName("heading");
coll1[0].innerHTML = "This is the top heading";
var coll2 = document.getElementsByTagName("P");
coll2[2].innerHTML = "This is the new third paragraph";
```

will change the HTML code to:

```
<body>
<h1 class="heading">This is the top heading</h1>
<p>This is paragraph one</p>
<p>This is paragraph two</p>
<h2 class="heading">This is the second heading</h2>
<p>This is the new third paragraph</p>
<p>This is paragraph four</p>
</body>
```

We will not cover all of the document methods, but here are a few others that may be useful:

- `createElement(tag)` creates a new element with the specified tag type. The tag argument should be a string with the tag name in upper case. For example,

  `var elem = document.createElement("H1"):`

  creates an element with the <h1> tag. The element may be given content by a statement such as

  `elem.innerHTML = "This is a heading";`

  The element created is initially unattached; it may be appended to the document body by the statement

  `document.body.appendChild(elem);`

  The last two statements actually make use of properties and methods of the `element` object, not the `document` object. It is also possible to place the new element at any desired place within the document. We will see how to do this shortly.

- `createAttribute(attname)` can be used to add an attribute to an element we have created, or to any other existing element. To add the attribute `class="myClass"` to the element created above, we could write:

  ```
  var att = document.CreateAttribute("class");
  att.value = "myClass";
  elem.setAttributeNode(att);
  ```

- `addEventListener(event, function)` defines a function to be executed when a specified event occurs. As a `document` method the event is associated with the entire document, not any specific element. For example:

  `document.addEventListener("click", function() { ... });`

  will cause the specified function to run when there is a click event *anywhere* within the document.

Complete information on these and the other properties and methods of the `document` object can be found in the W3C reference.

The Element Object

The `element` object represents a single element. This object has a large number of properties and methods, some of which may depend on the element type. In particular, `element` methods (rather than `document` methods) are used to navigate the DOM tree by finding elements by their position relative to other elements.

We will consider just a few of the more important properties and elements. Here are some properties that identify nodes related to the current node:

- `children`: returns a list of all the element nodes that are children of the object, as an **HTMLCollection**. The nodes are given in the order they appear on the page.

- `childNodes`: same as children but includes attribute and comment nodes.

- `firstElementChild`, `lastElementChild`: these properties return the first child node element and the last child node element, respectively, of the element object.

- `firstChild`, `lastChild`: returns the first and last child node, respectively, including attribute and comment nodes.

- `nextSibling`, `nextElementSibling`: returns the next child node with the same parent as the current node, optionally counting non-element nodes.

- `parentNode`, `parentElement`: returns the parent node of the current node.

Once an element or node is identified, a number of methods are available to modify or remove it, or to insert a new node with a specified position relative to the current node in the DOM tree:

- `getAttribute(`*attname*`)`, `setAttribute(`*attname, value*`)`: get or set a value in an element node for the specified attribute.

- `insertBefore(`*newnode, childnode*`)`: insert a new node just before an existing child node.

- `insertAdjacentElement(`*position, newelement*`)`: insert a new element before or after the current element, or as the first or last child of the current element, depending on the position string.

- `appendChild(`*newnode*`)`: add the specified new node as the last child of the current node.

- `remove()`: remove the current element.
- `removeChild(childnode)`: remove the specified child node.

The following methods add an event listener to a node or remove it from the node:

- `addEventListener(event, function)`: add the specified function as a listener or handler for the specified event associated with the current element.
- `removeEventListener(event, function)`: remove an existing listener from the current element.

Lastly, remember that the `innerHTML` property is used to get or set the content of any element, unless that element is void.

Many HTML element types have additional properties that apply only to those elements. For full details on HTML DOM elements, properties and methods see the W3C reference.

The Browser Object Model

The Browser Object Model (BOM) is a representation of some specific properties of the window displayed by a browser. There is no official standard for the BOM, but it is implemented fairly consistently by most modern browsers.

The core object of the BOM is the `window` object. This is the **global** object for all JavaScript programs that run in a browser. Unlike all other objects, properties and methods of the `window` object may be specified without the `window` prefix. This is why, in Chapter 3, we introduced the `prompt()` method (or function) without calling it `window.prompt()`. Even the `document` object is actually a property of the `window` object!

Two `window` properties give the width and the height of the current browser window in pixels, not including toolbars or scrollbars:

- `window.innerHeight`: window height in pixels
- `window.innerWidth`: window width in pixels

A few window methods control the state and position of the window itself:

- `window.open(parameters)`: open a new window. The parameters give the window name, the content to load, and other information such as size and position. Some of the details are browser dependent.
- `window.close()`: close the window.
- `window.moveTo(horiz, vert)`: move the window to the specified position.

The window object has several object properties that provide useful information about the window and about the browser itself:

- `window.screen` provides information about the window size, resolution, and color depth.

- `window.location` provides information about the source of the content being displayed, such as a URL.

- `window.history` contains information about the browsing history.

- `window.navigator` contains information about the browser itself, such as its name, version, language, and platform type.

Chapter 15: Related Technologies

More than most other languages, JavaScript is designed to work with partner technologies. The original purpose of the language, and still by far its most common use, is to bring interaction to HTML web pages through program code that is run by a web browser. Along the way, JavaScript has had to learn to interact with some other related technologies. In addition, some important systems have developed to expand the power of JavaScript to new uses and support easier development.

In this chapter, we briefly review a few of those technologies.

HTML and CSS

We have learned from the beginning that JavaScript is intimately related to the HyperText Markup Language (HTML) and is designed primarily to interact with HTML documents. For this reason, HTML was introduced in Chapter 2 and is described in some detail in Appendix D. We will not discuss HTML any further here.

We have also learned a little about Cascading Style Sheets (CSS), which were introduced in Chapter 7 and described more fully in Appendix E. The relationship between CSS and JavaScript is limited. However, there are two important things that JavaScript can do with styles via the DOM:

1. Elements can be located by their CSS selector. The method

    `document.querySelector()` takes a CSS selector as its argument and returns the first element that matches that selector. Similarly,

    `document.querySelectorAll()` takes a CSS selector and returns a list of *all* elements that match.

    CSS selectors are very powerful, so this enables JavaScript to locate a wide range of elements. For example:

    `document.querySelector("a:active");` returns the active link on the page.

    `document.querySelectorAll("input:checked");` returns all input elements that are checked.

```
document.querySelectorAll("p:only-child");
```
returns all `<p>` elements that are the only child of their parents.

2. The style of an element can be modified by JavaScript code. For example, if we define a button as:
```
<button id="btn1" onclick="setColor(btn1)">Push Me</button>
```
and our JavaScript contains
```
function setcolor(btn) {
    getElementById(btn).style.color = "red";
}
```

then the button will turn red when it is clicked.

XML

The next two technologies are actually variations of HTML. They have very little connection to JavaScript, but they are important members of the world of web-based notations.

The **eXtensible Markup Language (XML)** has become extremely widely used in recent years. XML is syntactically very similar to HTML, but its purpose is not to represent web pages, but to provide a method to define almost any type of hierarchically structured data.

The XML syntax is both simpler and stricter than HTML. It is designed to be parsed and unparsed by tools provided by various programming languages such as Java, C#, Python, and others.

Here is an example XML file based on the `composers` array example in Chapter 10. Note that each row, and each value within the row, now must be given a tag type:

```
<?xml version="1.0" ?>
    <composers>
        <composer>
            <name>Mozart</name>
            <birthyear>1756</birthyear>
            <country>Austria</country>
        </composer>
        <composer>
            <name>Vivaldi</name>
            <birthyear>1678</birthyear>
            <country>Italy</country>
```

```
        </composer>
        <composer>
            <name>Bach</name>
            <birthyear>1685</birthyear>
            <country>Germany</country>
        </composer>
        <composer>
            <name>Tchaikovsky</name>
            <birthyear>1840</birthyear>
            <country>Russia</country>
        </composer>
        <composer>
            <name>Dvorak</name>
            <birthyear>1841</birthyear>
            <country>Czechoslovakia</country>
        </composer>
    </composers>
```

Notice that the tag names are customized for the application. In XML you can use any tag names as long as they will be understood by those who process the file. Separate tools can be used to define the **schema** for an XML file, just as you would for a database. The schema is identified by optional declarations not shown above.

This example shows that XML is very verbose, but it presents data in a format that can readily be exchanged and understood by the great majority of systems.

XML elements may include attributes. These attributes can be customized and defined in XML schemas, just as the element tags are. For example, we may choose to add a `continent` attribute to the `country` tag:

```
<country continent="Europe">Italy</country>
```

JavaScript does not work directly with XML, but methods are available to allow JavaScript code to read an XML file as a string and parse it, producing a `document` object representing the DOM tree for the XML. The following code, supported by all current browsers, will read an XML string and return a structured DOM tree object:

```
var parser = new DOMParser()
var domObj = parser.parseFromString(XMLstring, "text/xml")
```

Conversely, the code below will take a DOM tree object and convert it to an XML string:

```
var serializer = new XMLSerializer();
var XMLstring = serializer.serializeToString(domObj);
```

XHTML

HTML has a fairly well-defined syntax, but its rules have become relaxed somewhat, especially with HTML5. In particular, HTML5 no longer strictly conforms to the specification for the original parent of HTML, the Standard Generalized Markup Language (SGML).

Because of this difference, there has been some interest in defining a version of HTML that *is* a strict SGML application, and can be parsed by system-independent tools. XHTML is a variation of HTML that follows HTML5 as closely as possible, but at the same time, conforms to XML which in turn conforms to SGML. XHTML documents still represent web pages, but they can be parsed (and error checked) more reliably by system-independent tools.

XHTML offers some important features but at the same time is difficult for many browsers to work with. This notation has not yet gained widespread use.

JSON

Another way to represent information that has become quite popular is the JavaScript Simple Object Notation (JSON). JSON is not a markup language; it is actually a JavaScript data structure. JSON is much simpler than XML (and therefore less expressive), but it can be systematically transformed to and from a string format that can be used for reliable data exchange.

Within a JavaScript program, a JSON object, like any object, is a collection of name-value pairs. All names as usual are strings. Values may be strings, numbers, booleans, or null; they may also be arrays or other objects. No other types are permitted.

Using the XML example above, to represent one `composer` record, we could write:

```
{
    "name": "Mozart",
    "birthYear": 1756,
    "country": "Austria"
}
```

Here we have chosen to preserve the XML names of the individual values. Two of these values are strings and one is a number.

To represent the complete set of records, we can store them in an array, which in turn becomes the value for a name-value pair in another object:

```
{
```

```
"composers": [
    {
        "name": "Mozart",
        "birthYear": "1756",
        "country": "Austria"
    },
    {
        "name": "Vivaldi",
        "birthYear": "1678",
        "country": "Italy"
    },
    {
        "name": "Bach",
        "birthyear": "1685",
        "country": "Germany"
    },
    {
        "name": "Tchaikovsky",
        "birthyear": "1840",
        "country": "Russia"
    },
    {
        "name": "Dvorak",
        "birthyear": "1841",
        "country": "Czechoslovakia"
    }
    ]
}
```

The outer object retains the name `composers`. Note that if we tried to retain the XML tag name for each `composer` record, we would wind up with an object in which every property had the same name. In XML, `composer` is a tag type, and many elements may have the same type. But we cannot have properties with the same name within the same object.

There are other important ways in which information contained in an XML document may not translate into JSON. In particular, there is no direct equivalent of XML attributes. If we need to represent the attribute `continent` on the `country` tag, as described above, we will have to write:

```
{
    "name": "Vivaldi",
    "birthyear": "1678",
    "country": "Italy",
    "continent": "Europe"
```

```
        },
```

This would preserve the attribute value, but lose the fact that `continent` is an attribute of the `country` element type.

AJAX

The next item to discuss is more a programming method than a specific new notation, but it does add an important functionality to JavaScript and some of the notations we have discussed already. **Asynchronous JavaScript And XML (AJAX)** obtains its name from a method for processing XML data *asynchronously* using JavaScript. The asynchronous part involves the ability to do (at least) two things at once. If a JavaScript program sends a request to a web server, ordinarily it would have to wait, doing nothing, until a response is received. AJAX enables the program to continue doing its normal processing while the server is processing the request.

In practice, what this means is that a browser can continue to render a web page, including handling JavaScript interaction, even while a request for data is being processed by the server. Often this request will result in a (possibly large) set of data to be returned as an XML or JSON file. The X in AJAX stands for XML, but today the data processed is equally likely to be JSON, if not more so. The JavaScript method that makes the request does not wait for a response. Instead, the response from the server causes an *event* to occur in the browser, which is processed by an appropriate event handler.

AJAX also helps enable JavaScript to update a portion of the page, such as a table, without the need to recreate the entire page. Only the changed portions need to be redisplayed.

In JavaScript terms, the key to the AJAX functionality is the js object `XMLHttpRequest`. This object can be used to construct a server request at a low level, including any necessary header elements. A typical server request using this object might be:

```
AJAXreq = new XMLHttpRequest;
AJAXreq.open('GET', URI, true);
```

This example assumes that the web server provides a REST style API using the HyperText Transfer Protocol (HTTP). Here 'GET' specifies the manner of access (read only) ; the **Universal Resource Identifier (URI)** identifies the server and specifies what data to get; and the Boolean `true` indicates that this request should be asynchronous.

The method above constructs the request. To actually send it we can use:

```
AJAXreq.send(null);
```

After receiving this request, the server will produce the necessary data and send it asynchronously to the browser (or client). The data may have the form of an XML string, JSON string, or a plain text string.

To provide the appropriate action when the response is received, the JavaScript in the browser should include a function definition such as:

```
AJAXreq.onreadystatechange = function() { ... }
```

The specified function will be executed when the data from the server is received.

jQuery

The last technology to be discussed in this chapter is **jQuery**. jQuery (not an acronym) is a package of JavaScript code that can simplify a lot of common tasks. Among the tasks that jQuery can help with are:

- Access the DOM tree elements using CSS-style selectors
- Update the DOM tree in simpler and more powerful ways
- Attach event listeners to DOM elements

Some of these tasks can be done in other ways. However, besides simplifying the syntax, jQuery helps ensure that these operations will work in essentially any browser.

For example, with the jQuery methods loaded, the statement:

```
$('p.class1').addClass('goodclass');
```

adds the value `'goodclass'` to the class attribute of every <p> element having the class `'class1'`. The dollar sign (`$`) is a shorthand for the main function, `jQuery()`. There is no need for a loop to process each element individually.

For full information on jQuery, and access to the latest version, see jquery.org.

Chapter 16: Beyond the Browser

JavaScript was developed for one central reason: to create interactive web pages that operate within a web browser. At this it has been enormously successful. The vast majority of web pages make use of JavaScript, and all major browsers support it. Since JavaScript is interpreted entirely within a browser, it avoids most of the security risks that came with the earlier Java applets. JavaScript is an essential tool in any web developer's toolkit.

A complete web architecture, though, involves web pages – usually HTML and JavaScript – running in a browser, but interacting with a web server. Indeed, the content for the web page must be delivered by the web server in the first place. After that, it is increasingly likely that the web server will be called on to run programs or access databases to supply information that the web page requires.

For this reason, the JavaScript within the web page may need to operate in partnership with programs running on the server. These programs may be written using traditional general-purpose languages such as Java, C++, or Python. However, they are often written in languages designed especially for server programming, including PHP, ASP, Perl, or Ruby.

Developers of a modern dynamic website, then, need to work not only with client-side (browser) technologies, including HTML, CSS, and JavaScript, but also with server-side technologies. Until recently this has meant learning at least one if not several new languages. But now there is a new language that is beginning to be used for server-side programming: JavaScript! If JavaScript can be used on both sides, there is a lot less to learn.

In this final chapter, we will look at how JavaScript may be used for server-side programming, and maybe for other purposes outside the browser as well.

Web Server Architecture

Just as the browser is the software package that runs on a user's computer to manage web pages, the web server is a package that runs on the server computer to provide web pages on request and to interact with them as the user requires. The most widely used web servers include Apache, Microsoft IIS, and nginx. These differ in many details, as do web browsers, but overall, they perform similar functions.

A web browser acts independently, usually controlled by a user sitting at the computer or working with a mobile device. The user initiates a request for a web page, causing the browser to send a message to a specific **IP address**. The message is sent using a standard web **protocol**, generally HTTP or the more secure HTTPS. This request also specifies a **port number**, and generally has various other parameters as well. This is a lot like calling a function, but on a different computer.

The web server listens for messages that arrive at its IP, but only accepts those that can be authenticated (such as with a password) and that include expected port numbers. The server then sends the message to an appropriate server program depending on the port number. For example, port 80 generally signifies a request for a web page. The server program responds by sending the requested page (typically composed of HTML, CSS, and JavaScript) back to the client computer that requested it. The page finally is passed to the browser.

In the early web, based on static web pages, that was usually the end of the story. Today, guided by JavaScript code and user interaction, the web page will probably make frequent requests for new information, which are packaged as HTTP messages and sent to the server just like the original request. These requests will generally cause programs to run on the server to produce the needed information.

These server programs may be written in any of the languages mentioned above, including JavaScript.

Breaking Loose of the Browser

JavaScript was originally developed solely to create interactive web pages. Over the years, however, it has acquired all of the features needed for a full general-purpose programming language. Is it possible, then, to use JavaScript to write programs that are independent of web pages?

All programming languages, as you know, need support software to do their job. First, for traditional compiled languages like Java or C++, a compiler is needed to translate the original program into an executable form that is ready to run. Second, an executable program still needs a run-time system to load and control it and to provide extra functionality it may require while running, such as library routines or operating system services.

In the case of an interpreted or scripting language, translation may be done "on the fly" when running, so the compiler can be eliminated but the run-time system is even more important. This is the case with most traditional server languages such as PHP, Perl, and Python.

For JavaScript, which is mostly interpreted, the run-time system is a part of the browser. Each browser contains a **JavaScript Engine** that provides the necessary support for JavaScript running within that browser. But how can we run JavaScript *outside* the browser?

Node.js

The answer, clearly, is to create a JavaScript runtime system independent of the browser. The package **Node.js** is not the first to do this, but it is by far the most successful. Using Node.js, JavaScript can be used to write server applications, or even some types of applications that are completely unrelated to the web.

Node.js is based on the JavaScript engine from the Chrome browser, called **V8**. It is not itself a web server application, but its usual use is to write web server applications. Using Node.js, web developers can write both client-side code and server-side code for their applications using the same language. There is no need to learn a separate language for server applications.

Node.js itself is a standalone open-source application that is maintained by the OpenJS Foundation and can be downloaded for all popular platforms without charge from https://nodejs.org/en/download/ . Node.js does not run in a web server, nor is it a web server itself; instead, a standard Node.js program is used to *generate* a web server, which can then be used to host JavaScript server applications.

Consider the following brief JavaScript program designed to run under Node.js:

```
var http = require('http');
http.createServer(function (request, response) {
    response.writeHead(200, {'Content-Type': 'text/plain'});
    response.end('Welcome to Node.js!');
}).listen(8080);
```

The first line is a Node.js method that enables the engine to use the built-in module `http`. The rest of this program is a call to the `http` method `createServer`, which listens on port 8080 for a request message, then builds a response. Here the single line:

```
response.end('Welcome to Node.js!');
```

128

provides a text string to be returned as a response to the request. In principle this response could be the output of an enormously complex JavaScript program.

If you have downloaded and installed Node.js, you can put this text into a file called `welcome.js`. You can then use a command or terminal window to type:

```
>node welcome.js
```

This command will start the server, which by default listens on port 8080 of your computer, which always has the local IP address 127.0.0.1. So if you then open a browser and type:

```
http://127.0.0.1:8080
```

You should see a page displaying the line:

```
Welcome to Node.js!
```

Node.js gives a developer access to the full JavaScript language – current versions support ES6 or higher – but some things are a little different. In particular, there is no DOM or BOM. This makes sense; you are not working with a document or inside a browser window. The objects `document` and `window` do not exist.

What Node.js adds, though, may more than make up for this. This includes a standard collection of library modules, including modules that provide:

- File operations
- Event handling
- Server creation (HTTP or HTTPS)
- Timer methods

For more information on Node.js see https://nodejs.org.

Appendix A: Reserved Words

This appendix gives a complete list of reserved words in JavaScript. These are words that have the form of valid identifiers but should not be used as identifiers because they have a special meaning in JavaScript. Even though some of these words are not technically reserved in all JavaScript versions, you should avoid using them as identifiers at any time to ensure that your code will be compatible with all browsers.

* These words are reserved in newer versions of JavaScript, beginning with ES5.

† These words were reserved in early versions of JavaScript, but not in ES5 or later.

abstract †

arguments

await *

boolean †

break

byte

†case

catch

char †

class *

const

continue

debugger

default

delete

do

double †

else

enum *

eval

export *

extends *

false

final †

finally

float †

for

function

goto †

if

implements

import *

in

int †

instanceof

interface

let *

long †

native †

new

null

package

private

protected

public

return

short †

static

super *

switch

synchronized †

this

throw

throws †

transient †

true

try

typeof

var

void

volatile †

while

with

yield   *

Appendix B: Exercises

Chapter 3

1. Write a statement to display your full name.

2. Which of the following literals are written correctly? What is wrong with the incorrect ones?
   ```
   a. 35
   b. 5,284
   c. 'Happy birthday'
   d. "The boy said "Hello""
   e. FALSE
   ```

3. Write the number 256,000,000,000 as a literal in exponential form.

4. Which of the following are valid identifiers? What is wrong with the invalid ones?
   ```
   a. piece of cake
   b. $100
   c. 2ndOne
   d. else
   e. thisIsAVeryLongIdentifier
   ```

5. Write the phrase "time of day" as a camel case identifier.

6. What will the following program print?
   ```
   /* This program prints "Hello" and "Goodbye"
   document.write("Hello");   */
   document.write("Goodbye");
   ```

7. Write a program that prompts for a line of input and then prints that line as its output.

Chapter 4

1. Suppose the regular price of a concert ticket is $7.50, but there may be a variable discount. Write a program that reads the discount as a percentage and displays the new price. If the discount is 10(%), the price should be $6.75.

2. Suppose in a restaurant `numberOfTables` is 50, `seatsPerTable` is 4, and `dirtyTables` is 10. Give the value of the following expressions:

   ```
   a. numberOfTables * seatsPerTable
   b. numberOfTables - dirtyTables * seatsPerTable
   c. (numberOfTables - dirtyTables) * seatsPerTable
   ```

3. In the following program, what will be the value of x?

   ```
   var a = 30;
   var b = 7;
   var x = a / b - a % b;
   ```

4. Suppose `ageSarah`, `ageRobert`, and `ageMiguel` give the ages of three people. Write an expression that sets `robertIsOldest` to `true` only if `ageRobert` is the highest.

5. What will be printed by the following program? What will be the value of `total` after these statements are executed?

   ```
   count            =              10;
   total     =      --count     *     3;
   document.write("Total count is " + total++);
   ```

Chapter 5

1. Suppose `color` is `"green"` and `day` is 17. Which of the following conditions are true?

   ```
   a. day <= 20
   b. color == "red"
   c. color == "green" || day > 20
   d. color == "red" && day < 20
   ```

2. What, if anything, is wrong with the following statement?

```
if day > 20 {color = "blue";}
```

3. What is z after the following statements?

```
var x=15; var y=20;
var z = y;
 if (x > 5) {
   z += x;
 }
```

4. Give the value of cheese after the following:

```
var cheese = "swiss";
var color = "yellow";
if (color == "brown") {
  cheese = "gouda";
} else if (color != "yellow") {
  cheese = "parmesan";
} else {
  cheese = "cheddar";
}
```

5. Give the value of stateName after the following:

```
var stateCode = 2;
var stateName;
switch (stateCode) {
    case 1:
        stateName = "New York";
        break;
    case 2:
        stateName = "New Jersey";
    case 3:
        stateName = "Pennsylvania";
        break;
    default:
        stateName = "invalid state";
}
```

6. Suppose highTemp is 60 and lowTemp is 50. What is the value of tempDiff after the following statement?

```
var tempDiff = ((highTemp - lowTemp) > 15) ? "big" :
"small";
```

Chapter 6

1. How many times will the body of this while loop run?

```
var num = 100;
```

```
while (num > 1) {
   num /= 3;
}
```

2. Write a `while` loop that will read and then print a series of strings until two identical strings are typed.

3. Rewrite your code from Question 2 as a `do while` loop.

4. What is wrong with the following `for` statement?

```
for (var count = 1, count < 6, count += 2)
   { statement block }
```

5. Write a `for` loop that writes the cumulative sum of the first 25 integers as follows:

```
1
3
6
10
...
```

6. Rewrite your answer to Question 5, using a `break` statement to exit this loop when the sum would exceed 100.

Chapter 7

1. Given the HTML code at the beginning of the chapter, why will the following reference not work?

```
value = document.getElementById("textin").innerHTML;
```

2. Suppose you have the following HTML page. Write a JavaScript file that would swap the content of the two paragraphs when the button is pushed.

```
<!DOCTYPE html>
<html>
<head>
   <title>Paragraph Swapper</title>
</head>
<body>
   <button onClick="swapPars()">Swap</button>
   <p id="p1">Hello</p>
   <p id="p2">Goodbye</p>
   <script src=swap.js></script>
```

```
</body>
</html>
```

3. In the "Find Squares" example, why can't we simply define the function as `findSquare()`, with no parameters, and get the input value with the statement:

   ```
   var inputNum = inform.textin.value;
   ```

4. The following statement sets the color of the identified element to red:

   ```
   document.getElementById("elem1").style.color = "red";
   ```

In addition, the following HTML button is given an initial color of green:

   ```
   <button style="color:green;">Push Me</button>
   ```

Using this information, write code to display a single button that changes color each time it is pressed in the sequence `"green"`, `"yellow"`, `"red"`. Show the body of the HTML page, along with the JavaScript function.

Project 1

Appendix D describes the HTML tags used to define simple tables. Set up a page to display a table of your favorite book titles along with their authors. The table should have two columns and five rows. Each row will contain a book title in the first column and the author's name in the second column.

Fill in the book titles in the first column but leave the second column blank. Write a JavaScript function that will be called when a button is pushed. This function should step through each row and prompt for the author's name. When the name is typed it should be entered in its proper place in the table.

A second button should be provided to allow the user to clear the table and start over.

Chapter 8

1. Write a function that accepts three numbers as arguments and returns the minimum.

2. What, if anything, is wrong with the following code:

   ```
   function getBlue() {
           var color = "blue";
           return color;
   }
   var myColor = getBlue;
   ```

3. What, if anything, is wrong with the following code:

```
function getBlue() {
        var color = "blue";
}
var myColor = color;
```

4. Write an arrow function that compares two strings and returns the shortest (you should be able to do this in one statement so you can use the short form!).

5. Consider the following code sequence:

```
var redBalls = 20;
let whiteBalls = 50;
{
   let redBalls = 30;
}
allBalls = redBalls + whiteBalls;
```

What is the value assigned to `allBalls`?

6. What, if anything, is wrong with each of the following:

a.
```
x = 5;
var y = x;
var x = 10;
```
b.
```
x = 5;
var y = x;
let x = 10;
```
c.
```
const x = 5;
var y = x;
x = 10;
```

Chapter 9

1. The following object is designed to help plan a vegetable garden:

```
var garden = {
    length: 20,
    width: 10,
    organic: true,
    fertilizer: "manure",
    plants: {
        lettuce: 20,
```

```
        tomatoes: 6,
        carrots: 30
    }
}
```

Write a statement to add a method that returns the total number of plants planned for this garden. use a `for ... in` statement to iterate over the properties of `plants`.

2. Write code to replace the lettuce plants listed in the `garden` object with 10 spinach plants.

3. What is output by the following code (assuming the given order is maintained)?

```
var result = "";
for (var prop in garden) {
    result = result + prop + ": " + garden[prop] + "<br>";
}
document.write(result);
```

Note that the last line may be surprising.

4. Show code to create a `Date` object for the date and time June 5, 2020, 11:15 AM.

5. Write an object literal for a `circle` object which includes (at least) two properties: its radius, and a method to compute its area using the rule that area equals PI times the radius squared.

Chapter 10

1. Consider the following code:

```
var numList = [22, 35, 17, 40, 83];
numList[10] = 99;
```

what would be the value of each of the following:

a. `numList[3]`

b. `numList[7]`

c. `numList.length`

138

2. Suppose an array `colors` is defined by

```
var colors = ["orange", "yellow", "green", "blue", "indigo"]
```

Write two statements to complete the spectrum by adding "`red`" at the beginning and "`violet`" at the end.

3. Use `forEach` to write a loop that iterates over the elements of the `colors` array in Question 2 and constructs a new array `colorLengths` containing the length of each color name string.

4. Consider the "2-dimensional" array `composers` in the text. Write code using nested `for` loops to search this array for the value 1840, using a `break` statement with a label to exit the search if the value is found. Assume this value may be found in any row and column. At the end, print the row index and column index where the value lies.

5. Write a function that will accept a `Date` object as an argument and return the day of the week for that date as a string (e.g. "`Sunday`"). Use an array to store all of the possible strings.

Chapter 11

1. The HTML framework for our demo pages, with colors provided via CSS, was introduced in Chapter 7. Add the `onmouseover` attribute to the `button` element in this framework to change the color of the button to red when the mouse or pointer is over it. It is not necessary to change back again when the mouse moves away.

   Use any JavaScript example to show that your framework works.

2. Repeat Question 1 using an event listener. The name of the event is `mouseover`.

3. What is printed by the following code sequence?

```
var running = true;
function func1(running = false);
function func2(document.write("Running<br>");
var ret1 = setTimeout (func1, 5000);
var ret2 = setInterval (func2, 2000);
while (running) {}
```

```
clearInterval(ret2);
document.write("Done<br>");
```

4. Rewrite the `factTable` function from Chapter 10, using `try ... catch` and `throw` to create an exception, then catch that exception if the limit is out of range.

Project 2

In Project 1 you developed a web page containing a table. In this project you will setup a table of garden vegetables that should be based on an array of arrays in your code. Each vegetable that you choose for your garden should have a row in the table giving its name, quantity, and the cost of each plant.

A text field should be provided to enter the amount of your budget, and a button should be provided on your page to compute the total cost for the garden. If this cost is over your budget a warning message should be given. Use JavaScript exception handling to catch and deal with any errors that may occur.

Chapter 12

1. Give the result of the following bitwise operations, each applied to the bit strings 1101001101011011 and 1001011100101101:

   a. &

   b. |

   c. ^

2. Use `typeof` to write a function that will add its two arguments, if they are numbers, even if one or both is in the form of a string. If either argument is not a number, the function should return `NaN`.

3. What would be the value of `pos` after the following code:

   ```
   var Gettysburg = "Four score and seven years ago";
   var Getty2 = Gettysburg.replace("Four score and seven", "Two
   hundred");
   var pos = Gettysburg.search("years");
   ```

4. Consider the following string:

```
"Aab c25 abc d371 qa99"
```

Which substring or substrings would be matched by the following regular expression?

```
/\w{2}\s\w\d{2})/g
```

Chapter 13

1. Write a constructor for the `garden` object described in Question 1 for Chapter 9. The constructor should include parameters for `length`, `width`, `organic` and `fertilizer`. The `plants` property should default to an empty object.

2. In Question 1 for Chapter 9 you were asked to define a method. Rewrite this method as a component of a prototype. Then use `Object.create()` to create a version of the `garden` object using this prototype.

3. Write a class `Garden` that encapsulates the constructor you wrote in Question 1.

4. Modify your prototype so the method is now an accessor (i.e., a getter).

Chapter 14

These questions are about the HTML framework described in Chapter 7, which is shown here again (slightly modified) for convenience.

```
<!DOCTYPE html>
<html>
<head>
    <title>JavaScript Demo Page</title>
<link rel="stylesheet" type="text/css"
        href="example.css">
</head>
```

```
<body>
      <script src=example.js></script>

      <h1>JavaScript Demo Page</h1>

      <form id="inform">
            Enter some input text:<br>
            <input type="text" id="textin">
      </form>

      <br>
      <button id="run_button" class="button"
            onClick="example(inform)">Run</button>
      <button id="button2" class="button"
            onClick="example2()">Push</button>

      <br><br>
      The output:<br>
      <p id="textout"></p>
      <br>
</body>
```

1. What is returned by the following?

   ```
   var coll1 = getElementsByClassName("button");
   ```

2. After the statement in Question 1, what is the value of the following?

   ```
   coll1[1].innerHTML
   ```

3. Write code to add the attribute `class = "heading"` to the main heading on this page.

FINAL PROJECT

For your final project, you are to create a website with two pages and several important elements as described below.

1. Your site should have an opening page for login. The user needs to type a username and password. It is OK if these are fixed and predetermined. When the login matches, the main page should be loaded.

2. The main page should include two elements: a to-do list and a countdown clock.

3. The to-do list should have the form of a table with rows that list tasks, how long they will take, and by what date they should be completed. Internally this should have the form of an array. Users should be able to add or delete tasks.

4. The countdown clock should enable users to set a target time and start and stop the clock. When running the clock should countdown continuously, showing the remaining time in days, hours, minutes and seconds updated every second. If the clock reaches zero, there should be a clear visual display to attract attention.

Appendix C: Solutions

Chapter 3

1. `document.write("John Michael Smith")`

2. a. correct
    a. incorrect (comma not allowed)
    b. correct
    c. correct
    d. incorrect (string enclosed in double quotes cannot have double quotes in it)
    e. incorrect (the literal false must be lower case)

3. `256e9` (or `2.56e11`, etc.)

4. a. incorrect (contains spaces)
    a. correct
    b. incorrect (begins with a digit)
    c. incorrect (reserved word)
    d. correct

5. `timeOfDay`

6. `Goodbye`

7. `var inVal = prompt("Enter a line");document.write(inval);`

Chapter 4

1.
```
var regularPrice = 7.50;
var discount = prompt("Enter discount as a percentage:");
var newPrice = regularPrice - (100-Number(discount))/100;
```

2. a. 200

   b. 10 (multiplication is done first)

   c. 160

3. 2.2857142857142856

4.
```
robertIsOldest =
        ageRobert > ageSarah && ageRobert > ageMiguel;
```

5. `"Total count is 27"`

   final value of total: 28

Chapter 5

1.
   a. true

   b. false

   c. true

   d. false

2. The condition must be enclosed in parentheses:

   ```
   if (day > 20) {color = "blue";}
   ```

3. 35

4. `"cheddar"`

5. `"Pennsylvania"`

6. `"small"`

Chapter 6

1. 5

2.
```
var lastString = "";
document.write("<pre>");
var newString = prompt("Enter a string:");
while (newString != lastString) {
   document.write(newString + "\n");
   lastString = newString;
   newString = prompt("Enter a string:");
}
document.write(newString + "</pre>");
```

3.
```
var newString = "";
document.write("<pre>");
do {
   lastString = newString;
   var newString = prompt("Enter a string:");
   document.write(newString + "\n");
} while (newString != lastString);
document.write("<\pre>");
```

4. The control statements are separated by commas.

5.
```
var sum = 0;
document.write("<pre>");
for (num=1; num<=25; num++) {
  sum += num;
   document.write(sum + "\n");
}
document.write("</pre>");
```

6.

```
var sum = 0;
document.write("<pre>");
for (num=1; num<=25; num++) {
  sum += num;
  if (sum > 100) break;
  document.write(sum + "\n");
}
document.write("</pre>");
```

Chapter 7

1. `"textin"` refers to an `input` element, which is a void element, and has no content (i.e. no `innerHTML`).

2.

```
function swapPars() {

    var p1String = document.getElementById("p1").innerHTML;
    var p2String = document.getElementById("p2").innerHTML;
    document.getElementById("p1").innerHTML = p2String;
    document.getElementById("p2").innerHTML = p1String;
}
```

3. The JavaScript file does not have direct access to the element names in the HTML file.

4.
   HTML:

```
<body>
    <button id="colorful" style="color:green;"
        onclick="change()">Push Me</button>
    <script src=change.js></script>
</body>
```

   JavaScript (`change.js`):

```
function change() {
   var nextColor;
   var currentColor =
   document.getElementById("colorful").style.color;
   switch (currentColor) {
```

```
            case "green":
                    nextColor = "yellow";
                    break;
            case "yellow":
                    nextColor = "red";
                    break;
            default:
                    nextColor = "green";
        }

        document.getElementById("colorful").style.color =
                nextColor;
    }
```

Chapter 8

1.
```
function min3(val1, val2, val3) {
        var min = val1;
        if (val2 < min) {
                min = val2;
        }
        if (val3 < min) {
                min = val3;
        }
        return min;
}
```

2. Missing parentheses in the line

    ```
    var myColor = getblue;
    ```

3. The scope of `color` is limited to the function. In the last line color is undefined.

4.

    ```
    var shortString = (str1,str2) =>
      (str1.length > str2.length) ? str2 : str1;
    ```

5. 70

6.

    a. Nothing wrong; the definition of `x` is hoisted

    b. Line 1 causes an error; `x` is undefined

    c. Line 3 causes an error; a `const` cannot be redefined

Chapter 9

1.
```
var totalPlants = 0;
for (var plant in garden.plants) {
  totalPlants += plant;
}
```

2.
```
delete garden.plants.lettuce;
garden.plants.spinach = 10;
```

3.
```
length: 20
width: 10
organic: true
fertilizer: manure
plants: [Object object]
```

4.
```
var myDate = Date(2020, 6, 5, 11, 15);
```

5.
```
var circle = {
   radius: 0,
   area: function {
            return (Math.PI * this.radius ** 2);
         }
}
```

Chapter 10

1.
   a.   40

   b.   undefined

   c.   11

2.
```
colors.unshift("red");
```

```
        colors.push("violet");
```

3.
```
    var colorLength = [];
    colors.forEach(lenFunc);
    lenFunc(item, index, arr) {
        colorLength[index] = arr[index].length;
    }
```

4.
```
    const ROW_MAX=5;
    const COL_MAX=3;
    var row, col;
    start: for (row=0; row<ROW_MAX; row++) {
        for (col=0; col<COL_MAX; col++) {
            if (composers[row][col] == 1840) break start;
        }
    }
```

5.
```
    function getDayName(date) {
        var dayList = ["Sunday", "Monday", "Tuesday",
            "Wednesday", "Thursday", "Friday", "Saturday"];
        return dayList[date.getDay()];
    }
```

Chapter 11

1.
```
    ...
    <button id="run_button"
        onclick="factTable(inform)"
        onmouseover="this.style.color='red'" >  Run</button>
    ...
```

2. This answer has two parts:

   a. add the attribute `id="button1"` to the button

   b. Add a `<script>` element at the end of the body:

   ```
   <script>
   document.getElementById("button1").addEventListener
        ("mouseover", () => makeButtonRed());
   function makeButtonRed {
   ```

```
        document.getElementById("button1").style.color =
            "red";
    }
    </script>
```

3.
```
Running
Running
Done
```

4.

```
function factTable(formId) {

    try {
        // Get limit value, throw exception if invalid
        var limit = formId.textin.value;
        var errObj = {message:"invalid limit"};
        if (!(limit >= 1)) throw errobj;

        // Initialize variables
        var val = 1;
        var fact = 1;
        var index = 0;
        var factTb = [];

        // Compute values and store them in an array
        for (var count = 1; count <= limit; count++) {
            factTb[index++] = fact;
            fact = fact * ++val;
            if (fact > 999999999999999) {
                break;
            }
        }


        // Now build the output string
        var result = "<pre>VALUE      FACTORIAL\n";
        for (var i = 0; i < factTb.length; i++) {
            val = i + 1;
            fact = factTb[i];
            result += val + "            " + fact + "\n";
        }
        result += "</pre>";

    } catch(err) {
        result = err.message;
    }

    // output the table
```

```
        document.getElementById("textout").innerHTML = result;
    }
```

Chapter 12

1.

    a. 1001001100001001

    b. 1101011101111111

    c. 0100010001110110

2.
```
function add2(arg1,arg2) {
   var num1 =
       (typeof arg1 == "number")? arg1 : number(arg1);
   var num2 =
       (typeof arg2 == "number")? arg2 : number(arg2);
   return num1 + num2;
}
```

3. 12

4. "ab c25" and "bc d37"

Chapter 13

1.
```
function Garden(len, wid, org, fert) {
    this.length = len;
    this.width = wid;
    this.organic = org;
    this.fertilizer = fert;
    this.plants = {};
}
```

2.
```
var gardenMethods = {
    totalPlants: function() {
        var total = 0;
        for (var plant in this.plants) {
            total += plant;
        }
        return total;
    }
}
```

```
var myGarden = Object.create(gardenMethods);
```

3.
```
class Garden {
    constructor(len, wid, org, fert {
        this.length = len;
        this.width = wid;
        this.organic = org;
        this.fertilizer = fert;
        this.plants = {};
    }
}
```

4.
```
var gardenMethods = {
    get totalPlants() {
        var total = 0;
        for (var plant in this.plants) {
            total += plant;
        }
        return total;
    }
}
```

Chapter 14

1. This statement returns an HTMLCollection containing both button elements

2. Push

3. ```
var att = document.CreateAttribute("class");
att.value = "heading";
var coll = getElementsByTagName("H1");
var elem = coll[0];
elem.setAttributeNode(att);
```
```

Appendix D: A Little HTML

The most common use for JavaScript is to provide a method for interactively examining and modifying elements on a web page. The overall web page is written in the **HyperText Markup Language (HTML)**.

HTML is the universal language for writing web pages and has been since the early 1990s when the "World Wide Web" began. HTML was developed as a special case of the **Standard Generalized Markup Language (SGML)**, which was developed in the 1980s to provide a standard markup system for printed documents. However, the latest version (HTML5) is no longer based on SGML.

The language is maintained by the World Wide Web Consortium, usually known as W3C. HTML4 is universally supported and became an ISO/IEC standard in 2000. HTML5 has emerged more recently and is gradually being adopted by most modern browsers. Our discussion will be limited to HTML5.

This book is not designed to teach HTML, but here we describe some of the most important features of the language. For a complete tutorial and reference on HTML see https://www.w3schools.com/html/default.asp.

What is HTML?

The HyperText Markup Language (HTML) is a notation system for "marking up" a document to indicate the desired appearance of its elements, especially when displayed as a web page on a computer screen.

The original idea of HTML was to allow web page designers to specify appearance details directly, such as font size, italics, or the position and color of buttons. More recently the focus has been on specifying the *purpose* of various elements (title, headings, selection buttons, etc.) while allowing the browser to decide on the exact appearance in each case. appearance information is now guided by element descriptors called style sheets (see Appendix E). HTML5, the latest version, requires that appearance directions be given only in the form of style sheets.

Web Page Structure

A minimal HTML web page that displays a simple greeting on the screen might look like this:

```
<html>
<body>
    <p> Hello! </p>
</body>
</html>
```

The codes enclosed by <> are HTML **tags**. An HTML document is composed of **elements**, and each element begins with a start tag such as <xxx> and ends (usually) with a matched end tag such as </xxx>. The content of the element, if any, goes between the start tag and the end tag. The content may include other elements. All elements must be properly nested.

The tags <html> ... </html> must enclose the entire page. Inside these tags we have the pair <body> ... </body>. This identifies the visible content of the page. Within the <body> tags we have only one element, the sequence

```
    <p> Hello! </p>
```

that defines a paragraph.

An optional section above these tags, marked <head> ... </head>, can provide descriptive information about the page, for example, we could write:

```
<head>
    <title>My own Web Page</title>
    <script src=jfuncs.js></script>
</head>
```

The <head> section is used for "header" information that defines properties of the page that are not in themselves to be displayed. For instance, the browser may display the optional <title> in any way it wishes, or not at all. This is also a good place for JavaScript *functions*, which will be triggered by some event such as a button click. But JavaScript code to be executed unconditionally should appear only in the `<body>` section.

There is one other tag, not shown above, which normally should be included at the very beginning of an HTML page, even before the `<html>` tag:

```
<!DOCTYPE html>
```

This tag is not strictly part of HTML, but it tells the browser to interpret the rest of the document as an HTML page. Moreover, in this simple form it announces that this is an HTML5 page. Earlier versions of HTML are identified by several other, more complex `DOCTYPE`s.

The `<!DOCTYPE>` tag is usually not mandatory, but it is a good idea to include it at the beginning of every page.

Whitespace and Comments

Whitespace in an HTML document is usually ignored. This includes spaces, tabs, and extra line endings. However, you should not end a line inside a tag.

HTML documents can also contain comments. A comment is a string beginning with the four characters `<!--` and ending with the three characters `-->`. Comments are ignored by the browser and may span multiple lines.

Tags and Attributes

With few exceptions, every HTML element begins with a start tag such as `<title>` and ends with an end tag such as `</title>`. The end tag contains the same name as the start tag, preceded by a slash.

A few elements are defined as **void elements**, because by definition they have no content. These elements have *only* a start tag. For example, the `<br>` tag indicates a break at the end of a line. It has no content and does not require an end tag.

Tags may have **attributes**. These are name-value pairs enclosed within the start tag. A tag may have any number of attributes. A few examples:

`<p id="firstpar">` assigns an id to a paragraph element.

`<a href="http://www.example.com">This is a link</a>` makes the content text a link that goes to the specified URL.

`<img src=images/mother.jpg alt="picture of Mom" height="100" width="50">` specifies a graphic image to appear on the page, provides a brief description

156

for the visually impaired, and gives its desired height and width in pixels. This is a void element and so does not require an end tag.

`<button onclick="jsfunc()">PUSH ME</button>` assigns a JavaScript function to a button, which will run when the button is pushed.

Some Common Tags

HTML5 defines slightly over 100 tags. A few have already been introduced. Here we will describe some of the most commonly used ones.

`<p>`, already introduced, begins a paragraph. Most ordinary text in a web page is composed of paragraphs. `<br>` has also been introduced; this tag is widely used to end a line or add a blank line.

`<h1>` through `<h6>` define various levels of heading. As with most elements, the appearance of these headings is up to the browser but may be guided by style sheets (see Appendix E).

`<ol>` defines an ordered (numbered) list. `<ul>` introduces an unordered list (with bullets). within these tags `<li>` starts an individual list item.

`<table>` defines a table. Within the table, `<tr>` defines a row, and `<td>` defines a cell within the row. Various other tags also apply to tables.`<div>` defines a major section of a document. This is often useful to define styles or specify JavaScript actions. `<span>` defines a more localized section of a document, often within a single line.

`<q>` introduces a brief quotation, and `<blockquote>` defines a more extended quotation.

`<img>` is used to specify a graphic image, as illustrated above.

`<a>`, as also shown above, defines a hyperlink.

A number of tags specify appearance properties intended to apply to a brief sequence of text. These include `<b>` (bold), `<i>` (italics), `<u>` (underlined), `<sub>` (subscript), and `<sup>` (superscript). `<strong>` and `<em>` (emphasized) are alternatives to `<b>` and `<i>` that let the browser choose the appropriate representation.

There are many more tags described in the W3C reference pages.

Some Common Attributes

HTML5 defines over 150 attributes that may be used with tags. Many of these can be used only with one or a few specific tags, while others apply to many of the tags described above. Attributes that can be used with any tag are called **global attributes**.

Almost half of the attributes defined are designed to define the response to events. This response will have the form of JavaScript code or a JavaScript function. These attributes have names beginning with "on" such as `onclick` (run when a button is clicked), `onload` (run when a page or element is loaded), `onkeypress` (run when a key is pressed), `onscroll` (run when a window is scrolled), and many more.

A few other commonly used attributes include:

alt - specifies alternate text to describe an image or other object. Applies to <area>, <img>, and <input>

class - defines a classname for one or more objects (see Appendix E). This is a global attribute.

height - specifies the height of an element in pixels. Applies to a variety of tags for which height is meaningful.

title - provides title information for an element. Not to be confused with id. This is a global attribute.

There are many more attributes described in the W3C reference pages.

Appendix E: A Little CSS

Appendix D has summarized the principal features of HTML, including the newer changes in HTML 5. As explained briefly in Chapter 7, early versions of HTML were designed to include instructions on the specific appearance of each element of a document. More recently it has been realized that the HTML tags should be limited to describing the *purpose* of each element, and the appearance or *style* of each element should be described separately. With this approach, the style of a document or a group of documents can be changed without affecting their functional definition. This has led to the definition of **style sheets** and the emergence of the concept of **CSS**.

CSS has been under development since the 1990s under the oversight of the W3 Consortium. CSS 2.1 has been a stable standard since about 2011. Newer features continue to be developed, but their support by all browsers is not guaranteed.

This appendix provides an overview of the most commonly used features of CSS. This discussion is based on CSS 2.1. For a complete tutorial and reference see https://www.w3schools.com/css/default.asp.

What is CSS?

Style sheets are collections of styles expressed in a special language designed to specify the desired appearance of elements in a web page. CSS stands for **Cascading Style Sheets**. We'll explain the *cascading* part shortly.

As you know, JavaScript is embedded in HTML documents between `<script>` tags. When the browser encounters a `<script>` tag while processing a page, it passes the content off to its JavaScript interpreter.

In exactly the same way, style definitions may be contained in style sheets embedded within `<style>` tags. For example, we can write:

```
<style>
     p {font-size: large;}
</style>
```

to tell the browser that every paragraph enclosed in `<p>` tags should be rendered in a `large` font size. If this code is placed within the `<head>` section of an HTML document, it will control the appearance of every paragraph in that document.

What exactly is meant by `large`? The truth is that is up to the browser. Every modern browser understands style sheets, but the browser is free to interpret them as it wishes. Ultimately, all appearance decisions are up to the browser.

Where do the Style Sheets Go?

The example above shows one way that style information can be added to an HTML document. If style sheets are placed in the `<head>` section of the document, enclosed in `<style>` tags, they will define the style (for the specified elements) throughout the document. This is called **internal style sheets**, and it is one of three distinct ways this information can be expressed. The other options are:

- **Inline styles:** this method allows style information to be given as an attribute for a specific HTML element, for example:

  ```
  <p style="font-size: large;">Some paragraph.</p>
  ```

  This example will apply the specified style only to the specific element it is defined in. This is similar to the original method of combining style and purpose information, except that the style attribute provides a systematic way to specify CSS styles. As we will see below, CSS provides other ways to apply styles to specific elements, so inline styles should rarely be used.

- **External style sheets**: this method allows style information to be provided in a separate file. This is the usual recommended use of CSS. Style definitions in a CSS file can be easily incorporated in a whole collection of documents, and a change to the CSS file can apply immediately to an entire website.

  To turn the example above into an external style sheet, we could create a file called `example.css`, containing the following text (that's all!):

  ```
  p {font-size: large;}
  ```

Within the `<head>` section of the HTML document, we would then write:

```
<link rel="stylesheet" type="text/css" href="example.css">
```

If you don't understand all of this, don't worry. You don't have to. The `<link>` tag is used only to invoke external style sheets, and it will always be written like this, with the appropriate `css` filename as the `href` attribute. As written here the `css` file should be in the same directory as the HTML file. In general, this attribute may provide a full pathname or, for a remote `css` file, a URL. The one thing that is fixed is that the file extension should always be `.css`. Note also that `<link>` does *not* have a closing tag.

It may seem cumbersome to use a separate file just to define one style as illustrated above. But we can do a lot more with style sheets. The complete example from Chapter 7 can be expressed as a `css` file with the following content:

```
body {
    background-color: lightblue;
}
button {
    background-color: lightgreen;
    color: white;
}
p {
    color: red;
    font-size: large;
}
```

This file defines style attributes for two element types (`<p>` and `<button>`) and a color for the entire `<body>` of the page. This illustrates only one option in the full CSS language. It is also possible to define style attributes for individual elements that can be identified in several ways:

- By giving them a unique id
- By assigning them to a class

- By referencing their position in the DOM tree

These and other features of the language will be summarized in the next section.

We will usually assume from now on that we are using external style sheets in a `css` file. But what if there is more than one style sheet? Suppose, for instance, we have both an internal and an external style sheet in the same document? This is where the term *cascading* comes in, as the browser will "cascade" through all the style information in the order seen and may replace one style definition with another for the same element.

Generally, this means that the browser will examine the external style sheet(s) first, then the internal style sheet(s), to get the style definitions provided for each element. Along the way, any new definition will override or replace the previous one, just as a variable definition for an inner scope in JavaScript may override the definition in an outer scope.

Finally, any inline styles for a specific element will override everything else. And if there are no style definitions at all for a particular element? In that case, the browser must rely on its own default settings.

Note that each style attribute found can override only the identical attribute for the same element(s). If a particular paragraph has the inline style:

```
<p style="font-size: small;">Some paragraph.</p>
```

while an external `css` file contains:

```
p {
    color: red;
    font-size: large;
}
```

the paragraph will be rendered in a small font size, and the text will be colored red.

CSS Selectors

A CSS style sheet (internal or external) is composed of one or more styles, also called **rule-sets**. A rule-set consists of a **selector** and a declaration, and a declaration consists of one or more **properties** which are name-value pairs. The entire declaration is enclosed in curly braces.

In the example style sheet given earlier, one rule-set is:

```
button {
    background-color: lightgreen;
    color: white;
}
```

Here the selector is `button`, which refers to all elements in the document with a `<button>` tag. The rule-set contains two properties, `background-color` (value `lightgreen`), and color (value `white`).

CSS offers many types of selectors that can be used to identify individual elements or element groups on a web page. Here are some of the most common types:

- **Select element by `id`**. If an element includes an attribute of the form `id="myelement"`, then that element may be selected by its id value preceded by the pound (#) sign, for example:

```
#myelement {
    color: green;
}
```

The `id` value should be unique within the page.

- **Select element by `class`**. Multiple elements may have the same class, and a single element may have multiple classes. The selector may apply to all elements of a given class, or only elements of a specified type. Class selectors consist of a class name preceded by a period, optionally preceded by a tag type.

    Suppose that a web page includes the following tags:

    `<h1 class="first">`

    `<h2 class="business coach">`

    `<p class = "business">`

    `<p class = "coach">`

    Then the selector `.first` will select the first of these tags; the selector `p.business` will choose the third (but not the second); and the selector `.coach` will select the second and the fourth.

- **Select elements based on a certain attribute.** The selector has the form `a[attr]` where `attr` represents the name of the attribute and optional value information. The selector `a[href]` will select all elements that contain the `href` attribute (which specifies a URL). It is also possible to make selections based on the value of the attribute.

- **Select elements by their relation to other elements**. For example, the selector `div > p` selects all `<p>` elements that have a `<div>` element as a parent; while the selector `ol::last-child` selects the last item of an ordered list.

There are dozens of other selectors. Among these are selectors that enable you to:
- Select input that is valid, or invalid
- Select elements that contain links of various types
- Select elements when the mouse hovers over them
- Select parts of a paragraph
- Select the root element of a page
- Select all elements

CSS Properties

There are well over 100 properties that can be specified in a CSS rule-set. Many of these are organized into groups that concern specific appearance characteristics, including:
- background properties, such as background-color or background-size
- properties of borders around elements, such as border-left-width, border-top-style
- properties of columns, such as column-count, column-gap
- font properties, such as font-size and font-family
- properties that control and support animation, such as position and color changes

Other Notes

CSS colors may be specified in many ways such as common names (`"blue"`, `"hotpink"`), hex values (`#ffc320`) or RGB values (`rgb(120, 200, 30)`).

Property values may be literal numbers or strings, or in some cases functions such as `calc()` which performs limited calculations.

CSS can specify that a text element should be spoken and provide characteristics for the speech.

Appendix F: Resources

Duckett, J. (2014). *JavaScript and JQuery*. Indianapolis, IN: Wiley.

W3schools.com. *JavaScript Tutorial*.

Retrieved Jan. 13, 2020 from https://www.w3schools.com/js/default.asp.

Haverbeke, M. (2018). *Eloquent JavaScript, 3rd Edition*. San Francisco, CA: No Starch

Press. Retrieved Jan. 25, 2020 from https://eloquentjavascript.net.

Rauschmayer, A. (2014). *Speaking JavaScript: An In-Depth Guide for Programmers*.

Sebastapol, CA: O'Reilly Media. Available free online at http://speakingjs.com.

Made in the USA
Las Vegas, NV
10 November 2022

59115332R00096